CRIMINAL LAW:

ITS NATURE AND SOURCES

MATTHEW A. PAULEY

Library of Congress Cataloging–in–Publication Data

Pauley, Matthew A., 1959-
    Criminal law : its nature and sources / Matthew A. Pauley.
        p.   cm.
    Includes bibliographical references (p.175)
    ISBN 0-918680-72-7 (cloth). — ISBN 0-918880-74-3 (pbk.)
    1. Criminal law — United States.   I. Title.
KF9219.P38   1999
345.73—dc21
                                                        98-37482
                                                            CIP

PUBLISHED FOR
THE BAGEHOT COUNCIL
BY GRIFFON HOUSE PUBLICATIONS

Distributed by GRIFFON HOUSE PRESS, INC.
1401 Pennsylvania Ave., Suite 105
Wilmington, DE 19806

CONTENTS

In Memory of

My Father, Adam

and My Uncle, Henry

FOREWORD

In this world's ever-increasing changes, nothing is more simple than the Law, and nothing is more complex. Like Dickens, the best and the worst of times.

It seems that present-day legislators, and some courts have made difficult what was reasonably simple. In the past, the intrigues of the law, difficult as they were, were understood. It is only in modern-day terms that those intrigues are complicated by so many legislative and judicial variations that the legal profession has become somewhat entangled. Enter: *Criminal Law, Its Nature and Sources.* Dr. Pauley has given us here a strong presentation, in easily accessible language, of even the most difficult issues. In a brief, effective and knowledgeable manner, he provides the reader with more than a basic introduction to the subject.

At first, the general reader may feel disoriented, but he is soon drawn-in and made to feel "at home" through real cases and humorous anecdotes (often created by the author) that explain the various principles of criminal law. In a step-by-step process, the reader is led to a deeper, more complete appreciation of the law, in all its complexity.

As complex as the law is, the expert manner in which this well-documented book is written (the kind of writing not always found even among persons practicing law) gives the reader a clear perspective of the subject. There are few law texts today which do that for the Profession.

The Hon. Joseph G. Golia
New York Supreme Court
September, 1999

AUTHOR'S PREFACE

The idea for this book originated when I was teaching "Criminal Justice in America" to advanced Government concentrators at Harvard College between 1990 and 1996. My plan then was to make it a primer for undergraduates aspiring to go to law school — an introduction to the criminal justice system and the fundamentals of criminal law.

Most of the book, however, developed in the last three years, during my teaching of Criminal Law to second- and third-year law students at the Southern New England School of Law. I have used the book with considerable success in supplementing the casebook in that course. As it now stands, this introduction to criminal law is suitable reading for law students and under-graduates, as well as for scholars, practitioners, and the general public. It attempts to use narrative, court cases, and hypotheticals to make the subject more interesting and the material more understandable.

I am deeply indebted to my research assistants, especially Bob Hennelly, Kevin Whitaker, Ingrid Waldron, and Karl Topor for their invaluable aid in preparing this book. I would also like to acknowledge my colleagues on the faculty of the Southern New England School of Law, and all the other students I have had in Criminal Law at this institution over the past three years.

Matthew A. Pauley
September, 1999

CHAPTER ONE

Introduction

Substantive criminal law is primarily concerned with defining and considering the mental states, acts, attendant circumstances, and consequences which are the necessary ingredients of each of the various crimes. For instance, what must the prosecution prove to have someone convicted of first-degree murder or manslaughter? What defenses are available to the defense counselor for these and other crimes? And if the accused is convicted, how and why should we punish him or her?

Criminal law does *not* require any background knowledge of criminal procedure — a subject which focuses on the constitutional limitations on police investigation of crime — although many law schools combine both subjects in one course. Nor does the study of criminal law require much background in civil — as distinct from criminal — law. And yet, it is useful to recognize that the same actions which can give rise to criminal sanctions may also make a person liable for a civil law suit, possibly for breach of contract but more likely in tort. For instance, if you punch someone in the nose, you may be sued for assault and battery, and if found liable, you may be obliged to pay damages, but you may also be prosecuted for a crime — assault, disorderly conduct, criminal battery, etc. — and if found guilty, you may be subjected to punishment in the form of a fine or imprisonment or both.

It is sometimes said that the crucial difference between a crime and a tort is that crimes are offenses against the *public* while torts, like breaches of contract or interference in property rights, are wrongs to *private* individuals. Moreover, criminal prosecutions are brought by the *state*, while tort, contract, and property actions are usually brought by private individuals or groups of individuals (like corporations which, of course, can sue and be sued as artificial persons).

It is necessary to say that civil actions are *usually* brought by private individuals, of course, because governments can also bring such actions. For instance, the SEC can bring a civil action when it suspects a violation of the securities laws. And the federal government can seek civil damages, including treble damages, for violations of the antitrust laws.

But can criminal prosecutions ever be brought by private individuals? In a fascinating little book on criminal procedure in Victorian Britain — the Britain of Charles Dickens — Frederick William Maitland, one of the greatest legal historians who ever lived, tells us that in the England of 1885, "any person can prosecute any person for any crime." But, Maitland goes on, any such prosecution is brought on behalf of the crown. And the crown has two checks on the prosecution — the power to stop the criminal proceedings and the power to pardon. The pardoning power, Maitland notes, is limited to criminal prosecutions. "The Queen cannot forgive a wrong done to one of her subjects or stop a civil action which he brings," he says.[1]

This last point is true in America today, as well. The President of the United States and the Governors of the states can pardon most criminal offenses (the President can pardon offenses against the United States — i.e., federal crimes — "except in cases of impeachment") but never civil wrongs. If one of your employees gets in a company truck and, driving recklessly down the highway, hits and kills a pedestrian, the Governor of the state might be able to pardon the driver and anyone else convicted of a crime like manslaughter, but no Governor or executive at any level could prevent the estate of the deceased pedestrian from recovering compensation from the reckless employee and/or the company.

Today, generally speaking, criminal prosecutions are brought by *public prosecutors* and on behalf of the state. As such, crimes are offenses against the public, against the common moral order. Is criminal law the same as morality? No. Of course, moral ideas have had a great deal to do with the creation of the specific criminal offenses. Murder and larceny and rape, for example, are crimes because society, through its judges and legislators, determined that such acts are morally unacceptable. But many acts which we might well consider immoral are not crimes. For instance, if you are playing tennis with a friend who is suddenly stricken with a heart attack and you make no attempt to get medical assistance for him and just let him die, this may be very immoral but in most states, absent some special relationship between you and the victim (it would be different if you were his father or mother, for instance), you would not be guilty of a crime. Similarly, some acts are crimes which may not seem particularly immoral at all. It may not seem particularly immoral to steal a loaf of bread if you are starving, but such an act is still a crime. A good *motive* is, generally speaking, no defense at all in a criminal case. Thus, if a man kills his wife — who is suffering from an incurable disease — because he cannot stand to see her suffer, we may pardon and pity him from the point of view of morality — we may say his motive was understandable — but, in most states, he would still be guilty of a crime.

There are some circumstances where a motive is relevant, however. For instance, if A's motive or reason for killing B is to prevent B from killing A, the law will not find A guilty of a crime. But it is important to see that morality and criminal law cannot be equated.

The study of criminal law is concerned with the definitions of the various crimes. Most crimes have several ingredients or elements. First, there is an *act*, or an *omission* to act when the law requires us to act. Lawyers call this the *actus reus* (Latin for "guilty act"). Then, there is the state of *mind*, which accompanies the act; lawyers call this the *mens rea* (Latin for "guilty mind"). For instance, degrees of felonious homicide (degrees of murder, voluntary and involuntary manslaughter, etc.) are distinguished partly by the mental state of the accused.

In addition to *actus reus* and *mens rea*, some crimes require certain *attendant circumstances*. In other words, certain additional facts must exist for the crime to happen. For example, bigamy requires a previous marriage, perjury requires that the witness be sworn to tell the truth, statutory rape that the girl be under age, burglary (at least according to the old common law definition) that the break-in occur at night, and so on. Also, some crimes require a consequence or *result*. Criminal homicide requires the actual death of a person; you cannot be charged with murder or manslaughter if your victim does not die. Arson requires burning of property. Other crimes do not require a final result like this. Perjury is a crime even if the false testimony had no effect on the outcome of the case. Assault is a crime even if the bullet you intended for your victim missed. Attempted murder and conspiracy to murder are crimes even if the murder never happens.

In addition to the particulars of the individual crimes, the study of criminal law is also concerned with more general issues that pertain to more than one crime. There are, for example, some general principles of criminal law that, in a way, pertain to *all* crimes. Generally speaking, for example, we do not punish bad thoughts, or punish something which was not a crime when it was done (the Constitution prohibits ex post facto laws), or punish someone who was insane when he committed the act, and so on. Then too, there are more specific principles that also apply to more than one crime. Self-defense, for example, may be relevant in the law of homicide and in the law of assault. Attempt can be relevant to homicide (attempted murder, for instance) or to other things (like rape and arson).

1. How Are Crimes Classified?

In English legal history, there were traditionally three types of crimes — felonies, misdemeanors, and treason. The reason for the distinction between treason and felonies was that the lands of a traitor were forfeited to the king, while the lands of the felon escheated to his overlord. In America today, where such forfeiture is largely unknown, treason is considered a sub-category of felonies. It is, to be sure, however, a very important and special felony — the only one defined specifically in the Constitution (see Article III, section 3).

The difference between felonies and misdemeanors is usually spelled out by statute. Generally, any crime punishable by more than one year in prison is a felony, and all other crimes are misdemeanors. But why should we *care* whether a particular crime is a felony or a misdemeanor? For one thing, many crimes are themselves defined in reference to another felony. For example, in a state that retains the "Felony-Murder Rule," if you accidentally kill someone while you are committing a felony, that is murder. Burglary is defined at common law as breaking and entering a home at night with intent to commit a felony inside the home. It may be justifiable homicide (not a crime at all) to kill someone to prevent the commission of a felony (especially a violent felony like murder or rape or kidnapping) but not a misdemeanor.

Punishments for crimes may be set forth in a statute in reference to some other felony. A conspiracy to commit a felony will be punished more severely than a conspiracy to commit a misdemeanor. And beyond criminal law, there are sometimes special civil penalties faced by a person who has been convicted of a felony — he may, for instance, lose his right to vote or practice law or serve on a jury — which would not apply to one convicted of a misdemeanor.

There are other ways in which crimes are classified, besides felonies and misdemeanors. Crimes which are bad in themselves are said to be *mala in se,* while crimes which are only bad because society prohibits them by legislation are *mala prohibita.* In many situations, it is difficult to say whether particular crimes are *mala in se* or *mala prohibita.* But violent crimes, like kidnapping or rape, would, of course, be *mala in se,* whereas driving on the left side of the road is *mala prohibita:* there is nothing inherently wrong about keeping to the left of the road — indeed, in Britain and Ireland and some other English speaking countries, it is the law to do so — and, in America, it is only a crime to keep to the left side because society has determined that traffic will keep to the right.

It may make a difference whether a crime is *malum in se* or *malum prohibitum.* If your conduct is bad in itself, and it leads to the death of someone, you may be guilty of manslaughter even if you did not foresee the death of the person. For instance, if you hit someone on the head with a hard shoe and your victim happens to have a very thin skull and suffers a hemorrhage and dies, you may be guilty of manslaughter.

2. *The Sources of Criminal Law*

In the beginning, all criminal law was common law. That is to say, it was made by *judges*. Judges, and not legislators, originally created and defined crimes like murder, larceny, rape, arson, burglary, and perjury in England long before the colonization of America. Even as late as the seventeenth and eighteenth centuries, English judges continued to create new offenses when the need arose and punish people who committed them. Conspiracy, for example, was created by English judges in the 1660s, shortly after the restoration of the monarchy after the death of Oliver Cromwell and while the memory of the violent conspiracies of the English Civil War was still fresh in everyone's mind. Of course, sometimes Parliament intervened to make some things criminal by statute: embezzlement and incest, for instance, were made crimes by statute. Still, for the most part, criminal law was made by judges.

In early America, many leaders urged a repudiation of common law crimes. Only legislatures, they said, were truly democratic; nothing should be a crime unless made so by the legislature. At the federal level, this opposition to common law crimes was largely successful. The reason for this lies in early American history. In the early days of the Republic, Federalist judges — judges who had been appointed by the Federalist Washington and Adams administrations — aroused the ire of their political opponents, the Jeffersonians, in Congress and in the White House, by creating crimes and punishing them. If this practice were allowed to continue, the Jeffersonians argued, there would be no limit to the power of judges to thwart the will of the people by putting their political opponents behind bars. By threats of impeachment and by appointment of judges who agreed with them, the Jeffersonians were ultimately successful in halting this practice. Even today, there are no federal common law crimes. A federal crime exists only if *Congress* says so.

But most crimes are *state* crimes. Even some of the most serious crimes are state crimes — murder, for instance, is a state crime, although murder of a public official (e.g., the President) could be a federal crime. Where does *state* criminal law come from?

The early American opponents of common law crimes were not successful in substituting legislation for the common law at the state level. Throughout the eighteenth and nineteenth centuries, American courts remained primarily responsible for creating, defining, and setting the punishments for crimes. Moreover, the states "received" the English common law of crimes as that law had existed at the time of the founding of the American colonies. Many states passed, and many still have on the statute books, so-called "Reception Statutes," declaring that the English common law, and English statutes "in aid of" that common law, which existed at the time America was founded (1607, when the first colony, in Virginia, was settled; or 1775, when the Revolution broke out) is part of the law of the state. So the states retained the old common law crimes of murder and manslaughter and rape and so on.

In the latter part of the nineteenth century and in the twentieth century, state legislatures began to enact more comprehensive criminal codes, covering most of the common law crimes and creating new ones as well. Some state statutes provided that nothing would be a crime unless found in the statutory code. Others retained common law crimes — allowed judges, in other words, to create or discover new crimes to punish ingenious people who think up new kinds of anti-social conduct which the legislature has not gotten around to declaring criminal.

Even in states abolishing common law crimes, resort to the common law by judges is frequently necessary to *define terms* in the statutes. A state statute may leave undefined a term like "steal" or "felony," and judges will look to the common law for the definition. They will, in other words, look at the way that word or term has been defined over the centuries of Anglo-American law.

Then too, where there are no common law crimes, there may well be common law defenses. If a state, for example, were to omit self-defense from its list of statutorily permissible defenses to homicide, a court would almost certainly hold such a defense legal in an appropriate case. Some states without common law crimes also have catch-all statutes, making anything that seriously disturbs the public peace or outrages public decency a crime.

There are arguments for and against common law crimes. On the plus side, it is pointed out that the legislature may not be able to provide by law for every possible anti-social act that could come up. There will be gaps in the law, and judges should be able to fill those gaps as the law arises. Thus if the legislature has not yet passed a law making embezzlement through computer programming a crime, a judge should be able to do so and punish the person who commits that act. On the other hand, it is said that giving judges such a power is undemocratic. And it is said to be unfair because people have a right to know, in advance, whether their conduct is criminal or not. As one contemporary text on criminal law puts it, to require a person "to study the criminal statutes (and the cases construing those statutes) may be fair enough; but to make him read the English and American cases on common law crimes and speculate on their scope is worse; and it is even more unfair . . . to make him guess at his peril as to what a court will hold in a new situation never before encountered by the courts."[2]

Although the common law continues to be very important, in filling gaps in the statutes and in interpreting words in the statutes, it is certainly true to say that, in America today, in every state in the union, legislatures and not judges are primarily responsible for defining criminal conduct. Until quite recently, however, many state criminal codes were a hodgepodge of statutes, sometimes contradictory and enacted in a piece-meal fashion. To remedy this incoherence, the American Law Institute (ALI) — an association of distinguished judges, lawyers, and legal scholars — undertook to develop a recommended model code. In the 1960s, the ALI adopted and published a Model Penal Code and Commentaries.

The Model Penal Code must be an important part of any law school course on criminal law. Many states have adopted it in whole or in part. In many others, judges will often look to the Model Penal Code for guidance in interpreting their state's code. Legislators often refer to the Model Penal Code in their debates about what conduct to punish as criminal and what penalties to set for various crimes.

In the chapters that follow, I will discuss principles of common law, interpretations of applicable state statutes, and provisions of the Model Penal Code, as they pertain to various crimes, defenses, and punishments. First, however, it is necessary to consider the ingredients of crime in more detail — the guilty act (*actus reus*) and the guilty mind (*mens rea*).

NOTES

1. Frederick William Maitland, *Justice and Police*, with a new introduction

by Henry Paolucci (NY: AMS, 1974), pp. 12-14.

2. LaFave and A.Scott, *Criminal Law*, 2nd edit. (St.Paul: West, 1986), p.73.

CHAPTER TWO

Actus Reus

One of the most basic principles of the criminal law is that thinking wicked thoughts alone cannot constitute a crime. There must be some kind of act, or at least an omission to act where the law requires a person to act.

Why is this so? In his *Commentaries*, Blackstone pointed out that "no temporal tribunal can search the heart, or fathom the intentions of the human mind, otherwise than as they are demonstrated by outward actions." Writing a century later in his *History of the Criminal Law of England*, James Fitzjames Stephen added that, if thoughts were punished, "all mankind would be criminals." In more recent times, commentators have asked "what would a system of laws embodying a rule providing for the punishment of intentions look like?" Images of an Orwellian state and multiple prosecutions for passing evil thoughts ("I wish my mother-in-law were dead!") come to mind. In short, thinking thoughts is not a crime. Generally, there must be an act.[1]

Bear in mind also that mere speech can be an act. For instance, in the crime of perjury, the act is speaking. A person who intentionally says "boo" to a man with a pacemaker may be guilty of murder if the man is so frightened that he drops dead of a heart attack; here too, the act (*actus reus* or guilty act) is merely speech.

But not all bodily movements are "acts." Only those acts which are voluntary are truly acts under the *actus reus* doctrine.

What do we mean by voluntary? The word voluntary is one of the most difficult and important in criminal law. It is especially difficult because it is used in different ways in different contexts.

The ancient Greek philosopher Aristotle said over two thousand years ago that an act is, in a sense, always voluntary unless its physical cause comes from outside the actor. So, for example, if a wind blows my hand into another person's face, Aristotle says, there has been no voluntary action. Or if someone reaches in my pocket and pulls something out of it, there has been no voluntary action on my part. But what if a person puts a gun to my head and demands my money? If I reach into my pocket and give him the money, Aristotle would say that my act is, in at least one sense, voluntary. It may have been coerced. I would not have done it if the man had not threatened me. But I was the one who reached into the pocket. I was conscious of what I was doing. In this sense, my act was voluntary.

It is this sense of voluntariness that we are talking about when we say that an act must be voluntary under the *actus reus* doctrine. Note that this is not necessarily the same meaning of voluntariness that we will encounter later in the book, in considering crimes like involuntary manslaughter. In the context of *actus reus*, a reflex or a spasm or an automatic knee jerk is not an act. But if a person, realizing he is about to fall off a cliff, grabs at something to prevent his fall, that is an act.

Consider the famous question posed by the modern philosopher Wittgenstein:

> What is left over if I subtract the fact that my arm goes up from the fact that I raise my arm?

If I say, "I raise my arm," this implies more than simply that a movement of my body took place. What more does it imply?

Now read the following case:

State v. Utter
Court of Appeals of Washington, 1971

Utter was charged with . . . murder in the second degree. He was convicted by a jury of . . . manslaughter. He appeals . . . . Appellant and the decedent, his son, were living together . . . .

The son was seen to enter his father's apartment and shortly after was heard to say, "Dad, don't." Shortly thereafter, he was seen stumbling in the hallway of the apartment building where he collapsed, having been stabbed in the chest. He stated, "Dad stabbed me" and died before he could be moved or questioned further.

[Appellant was a combat infantry-man in World War II. He testified that on the date of his son's death, he had been drinking very heavily. He had no recollection of killing his son.]

Appellant introduced evidence on "conditioned response" . . . [by a psychiatrist who defined it as] "an act or a pattern of activity occurring so rapidly, so uniformly as to be automatic in response to a certain stimulus." [Appellant] testified that as a result of his jungle warfare training and experiences in World War II, he had on two occasions in the 1950s reacted violently towards people approaching him unexpectedly from the rear.

The trial court ruled that conditioned response was not a defense. The major issue presented on appeal is whether it was error for the trial court to instruct the jury to disregard the evidence on conditioned response.

[Appellant] argues that his evidence, if believed, establishes that no "act" was committed within the definition of homicide: homicide is the killing of a human being by the act, procurement, or omission of another . . . .

What is the meaning of the word "act" as used in this statute? The word "act" technically means a "voluntary act." An "act" committed while one is unconscious is in reality no act at all. It is merely a physical event or occurrence for which there can be no criminal liability. However, unconsciousness does not in all cases provide a defense to a crime. When the state of unconsciousness is voluntarily induced through the use and consumption of alcohol or drugs, then that state of unconsciousness does not attain the stature of a complete defense. Thus, in a case such as the present one . . . the judge should give a cautionary instruction with respect to voluntarily induced unconsciousness.

The issue of whether or not the appellant was in an unconscious or automatistic state . . . is a question of fact. Appellant's theory of the case should have been presented to the jury if there was substantial evidence in the record to support it. We find that the evidence presented was insufficient to present the issue of defendant's unconscious or automatistic state at the time of the act to the jury . . . . The jury could only speculate on the existence of the triggering stimulus.

What if Utter suffered from "post traumatic stress disorder," a condition which some people suffer after a traumatic event such as military combat or rape? Should evidence of such a disorder be admissible? Should such a person be required to plead insanity?

We will return to these issues when we take up the insanity defense later in the book.

For now, consider the following hypotheticals:

1) During archery practice one day, Rupert Rumboy, whose aim is very bad, shoots an arrow into his instructor's chest, killing him. In a prosecution for manslaughter, Rumboy defends by asserting there was no *actus reus*. Held?

2) Suppose that Tommy Tomkins tells Dave Inchcape that unless Dave kills Alicia, Tommy will murder Dave's entire family. If Dave kills Alicia, can he plead absence of *actus reus* as a defense?

3) Same facts as above, except that Tommy hypnotizes Dave and tells him under hypnosis that unless he kills Alicia, Tommy will murder his family. What result now if Dave kills Alicia?

Aristotle also said that voluntary actions are the only ones that deserve praise or blame. Involuntary acts, he said, can only be pardoned or pitied. The Supreme Court of Washington put it very similarly in a twentieth-century case:

> An involuntary act, as it has no claim to merit, so neither can it induce any guilt; the concurrence of the will . . . being the only thing that renders human actions praiseworthy or culpable.[2]

Some crimes are specifically defined in terms of failure to act. Examples include statutes making it a crime to fail to report income on your tax form, or requiring a draftee to report for induction into the armed forces, or penalizing a motorist in-

volved in an accident who fails to stop. Other crimes may be
committed either by affirmative act or by omission. Murder and
manslaughter, for example, require the killing of a human being,
by act or culpable omission.

Consider the following case:

People v. Beardsley
Supreme Court of Michigan, 1907

Respondent was convicted of manslaughter . . . . His wife
being temporarily absent from the city, respondent arranged
with a woman named Blanche Burns . . . to go to his apartment with him. He had been acquainted with her for some
time . . . . On . . . Saturday March 18 . . . they went together
to his place of residence. They at once began to drink and
continued to drink steadily and remained together, day and
night . . . until the afternoon of the Monday following . . . .
On Monday afternoon, [a young man from a nearby hotel
who had come to the apartment over the weekend to deliver
bottles of whiskey and beer again visited the apartment].
During this visit . . . the woman sent the young man to a drug
store to purchase, with money she gave him, camphor and
morphine tablets. He procured both articles . . . . She concealed the morphine from respondent's notice, and was
discovered putting something into her mouth by him and the
young man . . . . She was, in fact, taking morphine. Respondent struck the box from her hand. Some of the tablets fell on
the floor, and of these, respondent crushed several with his
foot. She picked up and swallowed two of them. . . . Altogether
it is probable she took from three to four grains of morphine.
The young man went away soon after this. Respondent called
him by telephone about an hour later, and after he came to the
house requested him to take the woman into the room in the
basement which was occupied by a Mr. Skoba. She was in a
stupor and did not rouse when spoken to. Respondent was
too intoxicated to be of any assistance and the young man
proceeded to take her downstairs . . . . Skoba arrived [and]
respondent requested Skoba to look after her. [Later in the
evening,] Skoba became alarmed at her condition. He at once
called . . . a doctor [who pronounced the woman dead].

[Under] some circumstances the omission of a duty owed
by one individual to another, where such omission results

in . . . death, will . . . [constitute] manslaughter. [But there] must be a legal duty, and not a mere moral obligation . . . and the omission to perform the duty must be the immediate and direct cause of death . . . .

The record in this case discloses that the deceased was a woman past 30 years of age . . . . She was accustomed to visiting saloons and to the use of intoxicants . . . . She went upon this carouse with respondent voluntarily and . . . she had ample experience in such affairs . . . .

Had this been a case where two men . . . had voluntarily gone on a debauch together and one had attempted suicide, no one would claim that this doctrine of legal duty could be invoked to hold the other criminally responsible for omitting to make effort to rescue . . . . How can the fact that in this case one of the parties was a woman change the principle of law applicable to it?

The conviction is set aside and the respondent is ordered discharged.

Consider the following commentary on the *Beardsley* case, by a professor writing in 1958 in the *Yale Law Journal*:

> In a civilized society, a man who finds himself with a helplessly ill person who has no other source of aid should be under a duty to summon help, whether the person is his wife, his mistress, a prostitute, or a Chief Justice.[3]

In an experiment after the Kitty Genovese case, New York University undergraduates were asked to participate in what they were told would be two-person or six-person discussion groups in which each discussant would be put alone in a cubicle from which he could talk to the other member or members of his group by intercom. Without previous warning or explanation to the participants, the experimenters played a tape in which it seemed that another student was suffering a serious medical emergency in another cubicle.

The results were that 81% of those who believed that they were the only person who could hear the victim reported the emergency right away. But only 31% of those who believed that four other persons had heard the emergency did so. Why the difference? Does this explain the Kitty Genovese case?

Consider the following **hypotheticals:**

1) Mrs. Bennett fails to warn her son-in-law that her daughter plans to kill him. If the daughter does kill him, is Mrs. Bennett guilty of a crime?

2) Two mountain climbers, Mr. Chipps and Katharine, are by themselves, climbing in the mountains. When Katharine falls into a crevice, Mr. Chipps does nothing to rescue her and she falls to her death. Is Mr. Chipps guilty of a crime?

3) Mr. Chipps is 83 years old and suffering from acute liver failure. Without an operation, he will die. Is his wife guilty of a crime if she does not try to persuade him to have the operation and he dies as a result?

4) A husband stands by while his wife drowns her children (his step children) in a lake. Is he guilty of manslaughter?

5) Jane Austen takes her aunt, Agatha Bracknell, to her home and takes care of her for several years. When the aunt develops gangrene, Jane, sick of being a nursemaid, does not feed her or call a doctor. When the aunt dies, is Jane guilty of manslaughter?

6) Bryce Kelly, a powerful swimmer, starts to swim out into Lake Waban to rescue a drowning bather. As he gets close, he recognizes that the drowning victim is his arch enemy, Ernie. If Kelly swims away without rescuing Ernie and Ernie drowns, is Kelly guilty of manslaughter?

7) Ernie beat up Bob and left him lying on the road. Later, Dr. Morse accidentally drives over Bob and kills him. Is Ernie guilty of culpable homicide?

8) Defendant *accidentally* sets fire to a house, then fails to take any steps to rescue the people inside. Is he guilty of manslaughter if they all die? Does it matter if his refusal to act was motivated by a desire to collect the insurance money from the burned-down house?

9) Sam shoots Bill while defending his father from Bill's murderous attack. Sam makes no effort to call a doctor to assist Bill. Is Sam guilty of a crime if Bill dies?

10) A driver hits a dog with his car, then fails to stop and render aid to the animal. Is he guilty of the crime of ill treatment

of animals?

11) A woman places her infant child, poorly clad in freezing weather, outside on her front door step. Her estranged husband, seeing the baby, just steps over the child and walks out of the house. Is he guilty of "abandoning and exposing" the infant? If the child dies, is he guilty of a form of culpable homicide?

12) A helpless woman is hoisted onto a pool table in a bar and raped while spectators cheer. Are the spectators guilty of a crime because they did not rescue her?

13) Sally is chased down the street by a ferocious dog. She runs toward the closed door of a stranger's house. The stranger looks out the peephole, sees Sally, knows what is going on, and refuses to open the door. If Sally is killed by the dog, is the stranger guilty of a crime?

14) Bobby Aills kidnaps Amanda and puts her in the trunk of his car. He drives around for several days with his girlfriend, Betsy. Both Betsy and Bobby pay no attention to Amanda's loud screams for help. When Amanda dies from drinking window washer fluid, is Betsy guilty of a crime?

Next we turn to the other main ingredient of a crime — the guilty mind or *mens rea*.

NOTES

1. These passages are quoted in S. Kadish and S. Schulhofer, *Criminal Law and Its Processes*, 6th edition (Boston: Little Brown), pp. 180-1.

2. *State v. Strasburg*, 60 Wash.106 (1910).

3. Graham Hughes, "Criminal Omissions," 67 *Yale Law Journal* 590, 624 (1958).

CHAPTER THREE

Mens Rea

Beginning around the 1600s, judges creating common law crimes began to require that the criminal have a particular state of mind before he could be convicted of a crime. They used words like "maliciously," "willfully," "intentionally," and "fraudulently." As common law crimes were gradually replaced by statutory crimes, legislatures employed the same kind of language to denote what the law has come to call *mens rea*.

Today, some crimes require a **subjective fault** of some kind. For instance, if knowing receipt of stolen goods is a crime, this generally means that the suspect, to be convicted, must be shown to have *known* that the goods were stolen. It is not enough to say that a reasonable person would have known. The standard is subjective — what did *this* person, in his subjective mind, know? The standard is not objective — what would any reasonable person know? Other crimes require only **objective fault**. If, for example, a statute says that any person who "has any reason to know" that he possesses stolen goods is guilty of the crime, this generally means that the defendant can be convicted even if he subjectively did not know that the goods were stolen, as long as a reasonable person would have known. Finally, some crimes do not require fault at all. If a statute simply declared that "anyone who receives stolen property" is guilty of a crime, that statute could be interpreted to impose liability without fault, or what lawyers call **strict liability**.

The Supreme Court has said repeatedly that the "existence of *mens rea* is the rule of, rather than the exception to, the principles of Anglo-American criminal jurisprudence."[1] In other words, most crimes require *mens rea* or some kind of fault; strict liability crimes are the exception, not the rule.

But what exactly is *mens rea*? Oliver Wendell Holmes once said "most of the difficulties as to the *mens rea* [are] due to having no precise understanding what the *mens rea* is."[2] In a broad sense, *mens rea* is culpability or fault. But more specifically *mens rea* means the particular mental state or degree of culpability that is required for a crime in the definition of that crime. Not all culpable mental states may suffice for some crimes. For instance, if it be a crime to kill a person "intentionally," a person who killed negligently or even recklessly might be said to have a culpable state of mind, but he would not be guilty of the crime unless he was worse than negligent or reckless. He would not be guilty unless he killed intentionally.

Ascertaining what *mens rea* is required for a particular crime is not always an easy job. Some statutes are ambiguous. For instance, consider a statute that makes criminal "knowing selling of drugs without a prescription from a state-licensed physician." What does the word "knowing" modify in that sentence? If a person knows he is selling something but does not know it is a drug, is he guilty? If a person knows he is selling drugs but does not know he lacks a prescription from a physician, is he guilty? If a person knows he is selling drugs but does not know that the physician who wrote the prescription is not state-licensed, is he guilty?

To remedy this sort of ambiguity, the Model Penal Code attempts to define four mental states, any one or more of which can be used in the definition of a crime. Consider carefully the following excerpts from Section 2.02 of the Code:

> Except as [otherwise provided] . . . a person is not guilty of an offense unless he acted purposely, knowingly, recklessly, or negligently, as the law may require, with respect to each material element of the offense . . . .

> A person acts **purposely** with respect to a material element of an offense when . . . if the element involves the nature of his

conduct or a result thereof, it is his conscious object to engage in conduct of that nature or to cause such a result . . . .

A person acts **knowingly** with respect to a material element of an offense when . . . if the element involves a result of his conduct, he is aware that it is practically certain that his conduct will cause such a result . . . .

A person acts **recklessly** with respect to a material element of an offense when he consciously disregards a substantial and unjustifiable risk that the material element exists or will result from his conduct . . . .

A person acts **negligently** with respect to a material element of an offense when he should be aware of a substantial and unjustifiable risk that the material element exists or will result from his conduct.

It is important to note that, especially under the model penal code approach, there can be different *mens rea* requirements for the different elements of a crime. For instance, let us say that a statute reads: "whoever performs an abortion on a woman whom he knows to be under the age of 18 and whom he should know does not have the consent of either of her parents or her guardian for such a procedure is guilty of a crime."

This statute has several elements or parts. Leaving aside for one moment the *mens rea* requirement, for a conviction there must be, first, a performance of an abortion; second, the woman having the abortion must be under the age of 18; and third, she must not have the consent of her parent or guardian. But what is the mental state (or *mens rea*) for each of these elements? The first seems to impose *liability without fault*. The statute speaks of "whoever performs an abortion." It would presumably *not* be a defense for a person to say, "I didn't mean to perform an abortion" or "I didn't intend to perform an abortion" or "I didn't know I was performing an abortion." As the statute is written, even if no reasonable person under the circumstances would know he or she was performing an abortion, that would not be a defense. If the defendant "performs an abortion," that is sufficient, under this part of the statute.

The second part of the statute requires *knowledge*. If a defendant performs an abortion on someone that he honestly but unreasonably thinks is over the age of 18, that is a defense. It is a defense if he did not know she was younger than 18, even if a reasonable person would have known. The third part of the statute requires *negligence*. A person cannot defend by saying that he did not know the woman did not have consent (of a parent or guardian) if a reasonable person would have known. This is an objective standard. The state needs only to prove that a reasonable person would have known that the woman did not have consent.

1. Intent

One of the most difficult concepts in criminal law, indeed in all law, is intent. Note that the Model Penal Code does not speak of intent in Section 2.02. But many statutes do use the word intent. What does intent mean? How is it proved?

Consider the following case:

People v. Conley
Illinois Appellate Court, 1989

Defendant William J. Conley was charged with two counts of aggravated battery based on permanent disability and great bodily harm . . . . He was found guilty . . . of aggravated battery based solely on permanent dis-ability . . . . On appeal, it is contended that . . . the state failed to prove beyond a reasonable doubt that the victim incurred a permanent disability and that the defendant intended to inflict a permanent disability . . . .

The charges stem from events which occurred at a party, attended by two hundred high-school students, [with "unlimited beer."] One of those students, Sean O'Connell, attended the party with several friends. At some point during the party, Sean's group was approached by a group of twenty boys who apparently thought that someone in Sean's group had said something derogatory. Sean's group denied [this] . . . and said they did not want any trouble. Shortly afterward, Sean and his friends decided to leave and began walking to their car . . . . A group of people were walking . . . across the street when someone from that group shouted, "There's those guys from the party." Someone . . . from that group . . . approached Sean, who had been walking with his friend Marty Carroll . . . . That individual demanded that Marty give him a can of beer . . . . Marty refused, and the individual struck Sean in the face with a wine bottle, causing Sean to fall to the ground. The offender attempted to hit Marty, but missed as Marty was able to duck. Sean had sustained broken upper and lower jaws and four broken bones . . . . Sean lost one tooth and had root canal surgery . . . . Expert testimony revealed that Sean had a permanent condition called mucosal mouth and permanent partial numbness in one lip . . . . At trial . . . Marty Carroll identified Conley as the offender.

The defendant initially contends on appeal that the State failed to prove beyond a reasonable doubt that Sean O'Connell incurred a permanent disability. [The state criminal code provides that] "a person who, in committing a battery, intentionally or knowingly causes great bodily harm, or permanent disability or disfigurement, commits aggravated battery." The defendant maintains . . . that there is no evidence as to how [Sean's] injuries are disabling because there was no testimony of any tasks that can no longer be performed as a result of these injuries . . . .

The function of the courts in construing statutes is to ascertain . . . the intent of the legislature. The starting point for this task is the language itself, and the language should be given its plain and ordinary meaning. The defendant urges . . . [that disability means] an "inability to do something." The state [says the term disability is broader and can mean any] "condition that incapacitates in any way."

In arriving at a definition, however, it is also proper to consider the statute's purpose . . . . It seems apparent that for an injury to be deemed disabling, all that must be shown is that the victim is no longer whole, such that the injured bodily portion . . . no longer serves the body in the same manner . . . . [In this case, there was evidence of permanent disability.]

The defendant further argues that the State failed to prove beyond a reasonable doubt that he intended to inflict any permanent disability. The thrust of defendant's argument is that [under the statute], a person must intend to bring about the particular harm defined in the statute. The defendant asserts that while it may be inferred from his conduct that he intended to cause harm, it does not follow that he intended to cause permanent disability. The state contends it is not necessary that the defendant intended to bring about the particular injuries that resulted. The state maintains that it met its burden by showing that the defendant intentionally struck Sean . . . .

The relevant statutes state:

A person intends . . . to accomplish a result or engage in conduct . . . defining the offense, when his conscious objective or purpose is to accomplish this result or engage in that conduct . . . .

A person knows . . . the result of his conduct . . . when he is consciously aware that such result is practically certain to be caused by his conduct . . . . Because the offense [aggravated battery] is defined in terms of result, the State has the burden of proving beyond a reasonable doubt that the defendant either had a "conscious objective" to achieve the harm defined, or that the defendant was "consciously aware" that the harm defined was "practically certain to be caused by his conduct."

[There is an] ordinary presumption that one intends the natural and probable consequences of his actions . . . . Intent can be inferred from the surrounding circumstances, the offender's words, the weapons used, and the force of the blow. As the defendant's theory of the case was mistaken identity, there was no evidence introduced negating the presumption of intent . . . . The use of a bottle, the absence of warning and the force of the blow are facts from which the jury could reasonably infer the intent to cause permanent disability. Therefore, we find the evidence sufficient to support a finding of intent to cause permanent disability beyond a reasonable doubt.

Intent is a difficult term, in part, because it can apply to different things. A person can intentionally engage in specific conduct. Or a person can intend a particular result of his conduct. If I pull out a gun and shoot it, it might well be said that I am shooting intentionally. As long as I know what I am doing and as long as I am doing it (no one is holding my fingers on the trigger; I am doing the shooting and know it) then, in a sense, I am *shooting* intentionally. But to say that I am *killing* intentionally if one of my shots hits and kills a person means a different sort of intent. It means that I intended to kill that person. In other words, the death of that person was the intended *result* of my actions.

Under the traditional principles of common law, applicable in the law of torts and in criminal law where the model-penal-code approach has *not* been adopted, a person intends the *result* of his or her action either when he consciously desires that result (what the Model Penal Code calls *purpose*) or when he knows that this result is practically certain to follow from his action (what the Model Penal Code calls *knowledge*). For instance, if I shoot at a crowd hoping that I will not hit anyone but knowing that I almost certainly will hit and kill someone, I am killing intentionally under this approach.

The Model Penal Code, by contrast, distinguishes between purpose and knowledge. Although the Code does not use the word intent in section 2.02, a state following the Model Code would be likely to define intent (in the sense of intent to cause a result) as synonymous with purpose. A person, in other words, must have a conscious objective to cause a particular result. It is not enough that he or she knows that such a result is going to occur.

One may ask why a distinction between purpose (intent) and knowledge matters. After all, for example, a person is guilty of intentional murder if he shoots at someone *knowing* that he will kill him, even if it is not his *purpose* to cause the death. There are, however, some crimes that require purpose as distinct from knowledge. An attempted murder, for example, generally requires that you intended to murder — in other words, that your conscious purpose was to cause death. Knowledge usually is not enough. So, in a famous example with obvious contemporary relevance, if I put a bomb on a plane in order to blow up the plane and I know that people on the plane will certainly be killed if the plane blows up but I hope that they will somehow survive (my purpose, in other words, is to destroy the plane, not to kill the people), then if the bomb does go off and the people are killed, I am guilty of murder (knowledge is enough for murder) but if the plane does not blow up, I am *not* guilty of attempted murder because it was not my purpose to kill anyone.

Like intent, knowledge has been defined in different ways by different courts. Note that the model-penal-code approach to knowledge does not require 100% certainty, but it does require "practical certainty." But does it always? Like the common law, the Code recognizes the doctrine of "willful blindness" — the idea that sometimes "deliberate ignorance and positive knowledge are equally culpable." For instance, suppose that a man places a suitcase which he knows probably contains illegal drugs in the trunk of his car and drives from Mexico across the U.S. border. Can he be arrested for "knowingly transporting contraband"? Courts will sometimes use the doctrine of "willful blindness" in a case like this to find him guilty. As the Model Penal Code puts it, knowledge in such a case is established "if a person is aware of a high probability [of the existence of the relevant fact] . . . unless he actually believes that it does not exist."[3]

Does this solve the problem? Suppose you are sitting on the beach when you see TWA Flight 800 explode and crash into the Atlantic Ocean. In the words of the Model Code, you are aware that it is "highly probable" that there are no survivors. You do not believe there are any survivors. But do you *know* there are no survivors? Is it possible that some cautious people never "know" anything because they always have doubts? If you are standing in Dealey Plaza on November 22, 1963 and you see Lee Harvey Oswald leaning out of the window at the book depository with a rifle in his hand and two seconds later you see President Kennedy collapse from a bullet wound, do you *know* that Oswald has shot Kennedy? One law professor has said that a person does not "know" a fact "if he entertains any doubts about the validity of his judgment, and even when one is certain that he is correct . . . [he does not have knowledge] if additional evidence is available to confirm or refute his conclusion."[4] Is it possible that a person who did not know but was only *negligent* could be convicted under a statute requiring knowledge —because a reasonable person would have made a further inspection and learned more?

In addition to problems of what is knowledge and the differences between intent and knowledge, questions of unintended consequences of intended acts often come up. These will be dealt with more in subsequent sections, but an overview of them is useful now. Suppose A aims a gun at B and shoots but misses B and kills C. Under the doctrine of transferred intent, A is also guilty of murdering C. The reason for the doctrine is often said to be that, without it, A could not be prosecuted for the killing he intended. Transferred intent is thus a legal fiction, used to ensure a just result: when an individual with bad aim kills the wrong person, he is just as culpable, and should be punished just as much as if he had hit his intended victim.

Consider the following hypothetical:

Jim Featherstone is furious with his wife, whom he suspects of having an affair. He confronts her when she is sitting in the car with their teenage daughter. Pointing a gun directly at his wife, Featherstone pulls the trigger at least twice. One bullet hits his wife in the arm, the other hits the daughter in the leg. Can Featherstone be convicted of *two* counts of attempted murder — of attempted murder of both the wife and the daughter? If the first bullet had struck the wife in the arm but the second had struck the daughter in the head, killing the daughter, could he be guilty of attempted murder of the wife and murder of the daughter?

Consider this hypothetical:

Jim throws a rock at Professor Pauley, intending to injure him with it. Professor Pauley, quick escape artist that he is, ducks and the rock sails over his head, striking and smashing a window of a car nearby. Can Jim be convicted of "malicious and intentional injury to property"?

Other problems of unintended results arise as issues of causation. For example, suppose that A shoots at B, intending to kill him. A misses, but the shot so frightens B that he has a heart attack. While in the hospital recuperating from the heart attack, B develops a form of pneumonia caused by lying in bed too long. If B dies, is A guilty of murder?

Then too there may be multiple or conditional intentions. Sometimes these do not exclude liability. For instance, if a person breaks into my house with the intention to kill me if he finds me at home, he is guilty of burglary (breaking and entering with intent to commit a felony inside). But if a person takes my property with the intention to return it if it turns out to be mine and keep it if it is his, then he is probably not guilty of larceny (intentionally taking and carrying away the personal property of another). As the Model Penal Code puts it, "when a particular purpose is an element of an offense, the element is established although such purpose is conditional, unless the condition negatives the harm or evil sought to be prevented by the law defining the offense."[5]

Suppose that during a bank robbery, robber John Clay takes Sherlock Holmes as a hostage and, putting a knife to Holmes's throat, threatens to kill Holmes if anyone calls the police. Is Clay guilty of assault with *intent to kill*? Does it matter that he only intended to kill Holmes *if* someone called the police?

Note that assault with intent to kill would be a **specific intent crime** — a crime for which the defendant must be shown to have intended some future act or consequence of his illegal act, here the assault. Assault would be a **general intent crime**.

How does the prosecution *prove* what a defendant's intent was? A murderer, for example, does not usually keep a diary in which he writes, "Today I'm going to kill X." His intent must be inferred or gathered from his words and actions at the time. We saw that, in the *Conley* case, the court speaks of an "ordinary presumption that a person intends the natural and probable consequences of his acts." But actually the U.S. Supreme Court has held that it is *unconstitutional* for a judge to instruct a jury that "the law presumes that a person intends the ordinary consequences of his voluntary acts." Why? Because this may give jurors the impression that they *have to* conclude that there was intent, not only that they *may* so conclude. The rule about natural and probable consequences is a **permissive inference** not a mandatory presumption. If a juror is presented with evidence that O.J. Simpson stabbed his ex-wife in the neck with a knife and he/she believes that evidence, the juror *may*, but need not, infer that O.J. must have intended to kill her, since death is the natural and probable consequence of such an act. To say that the juror *must* so conclude — to say, in other words, that the law "presumes" there was intent to kill — would be to shift the burden of proof from the prosecution to the defense. It would be, in effect, to say that, unless the defense convinces you otherwise, you must find he intended to kill her. That would be unconstitutional, the Court said, because the due process clause requires that the prosecution prove every element of every crime beyond a reasonable doubt.

Finally, what is the difference between intent and *motive*? It is often said that motive is irrelevant in criminal law. That is not perfectly true. It is true that, for most purposes, the state does not have to prove bad motive in a homicide case. But even in a homicide case, motive may be relevant to guilt or innocence. If the defense argues that the killing was self-defense, the court will have to decide whether the reason for the killing (motive?) was self-defense. We will see more about the relationship of motive to self-defense later. As to motive and intent, consider the possibility that motive is, in many cases, just a secondary intent. For instance, if I shoot you to kill you so that I will inherit your money, killing you is my intent and inheriting the money (secondary intent) is my motive. In such a case, the prosecution might want to show motive — to prove that I actually did intend to kill you. But the prosecution would not be compelled by law to prove motive. Only intent would be required.

2. Recklessness and Negligence

Most definitions of negligence stipulate some degree of risk which the defendant's conduct must create and say that his conduct is to be judged by an **objective** (not a subjective) **standard**. For example, in the law of torts, a person is often said to act negligently when his action poses an unreasonable or unjustifiable risk of harm to others. Practically everything we do poses *some* risk to others. Every time we drive a car or turn on the stove, we create some risk. But the law does not call these actions negligent because the risk is so small. Even speeding in a car may not be unreasonable if you are rushing a person to a hospital. The reasonableness of the risk taking, in other words, is a function of how great the risk is and how socially useful or necessary the actor's conduct is. And a person is negligent even if he is not personally aware that his conduct is posing an unreasonable risk, as long as a reasonable person would be so aware. That is what is meant when we say that the standard is *objective*.

So much for negligence in tort law. What about negligence in criminal law? It is generally agreed that criminal negligence ordinarily requires *something more* than tort negligence. But what is the "something more"? There are two possibilities. The law could require that the risk be greater — not just an unreasonable risk but a very unreasonable risk. Or the law could require that the person be *subjectively* aware of the unreasonable risk, not just that a reasonable person would be aware.

In one famous case decided by Oliver Wendell Holmes when he was sitting on the Supreme Judicial Court (SJC) of Massachusetts, criminality was found based on very unreasonable risk *without* subjective awareness. The defendant, who was not a doctor, tried to cure a sick woman by wrapping her in rags soaked in kerosene. This caused severe burns, and she died. The trial judge told the jury that the defendant was guilty of manslaughter if his conduct created a very great risk of her death, whether he realized the risk or not. After conviction, the defendant appealed, contending that he could not be guilty unless he was subjectively aware of the risk. But the SJC affirmed the conviction. The risk, in other words, would have to be very great — greater, probably, than that required for tort liability — but the prosecution would not have to prove that the defendant was aware of the risk, only that a reasonable person would have been.

Note that the Model Penal Code solves the subjective/objective dilemma by distinguishing between **recklessness**, which requires subjective awareness of great risk, and **negligence**, which requires only that a reasonable person would have been aware of such a great risk.

Like intent, subjective realization of risk must sometimes be inferred from words or actions. In the English case of *Regina v. Faulkner* (1877), the defendant sailor, trying to steal some rum on board ship, lit a match to see the rum and caused a fire which destroyed the ship. He was charged with "maliciously setting fire to the ship (arson)," and the court, on appeal, held that there was no such crime unless the defendant knew there was a great risk of such a consequence. It might be said that the seaman probably did not realize how great the risk was that he would cause a fire because, if he had, he would have expected to be killed. On the other hand, sometimes people take risks with their own lives and simply do not care what risk they are also posing to the lives and property of others. In such circumstances, it seems perfectly acceptable to call their conduct reckless.

Recklessness differs from knowledge in that knowledge requires practical certainty while recklessness requires awareness of risk. But how great a risk must it be? Some have said that if the social utility of what you are doing is very low or non-existent, even a tiny risk may make one reckless. Suppose for example that there are 5,000 guns on the table, only one of which is loaded. If, not knowing which gun is loaded, I pick up one of them for fun and shoot it at your head, thus killing you, I may be held to have acted recklessly because, even though there was only a one-in-5000 chance that the gun I selected was loaded, still there is no social utility in my act and so my risk taking was very unreasonable.

Should the law require subjective awareness of risk for conviction of a crime, or should it be enough if the prosecution can show that a reasonable person would have been aware (the objective standard)? Critics of the objective approach say that a person cannot be deterred from risk taking when he does not know the risk. Also, they say it is unjust to punish a person when he or she, for whatever reason, really does not know the risk his or her actions pose to others.

Consider again the case of the kerosene-soaked woman. Certainly any reasonable person would know that wrapping a person in rags soaked in kerosene poses a grave risk of injury from fire and burning. But the defendant did not know that risk. Or, to put it more precisely, the prosecution could not (or at least did not) *prove* that the defendant was aware of that risk. If the defendant really did not know the risk, can punishing him deter him or people like him from doing things like that again? Perhaps it can. The defendant and people like him may not realize how great a risk they are posing; they may not think there is much of a risk at all. But punishing him may encourage him and others to think harder, next time, about what risks they *may* be causing to others. Is it unjust to punish the defendant who didn't know the risk? Perhaps, yes! But perhaps he is responsible and culpable, not for ignoring a risk he perceived but for failing to perceive a risk he should have perceived. There's always another way to look at it.

We will see a great deal more about subjective and objective standards of risk taking in criminal law. For now, just remember that the first three mental states of the Model Penal Code — purpose, knowledge, and recklessness — all are *subjective*. That is, all three ask something about the defendant's actual subjective state of mind; all three require the prosecution to prove what was in the defendant's mind — what his purpose was, what he knew, and so on. Negligence, as defined by the Model Penal Code, requires only an objective standard — what would a reasonable person have known. Subjective fault is usually said to be worse than objective fault. If you are aware of a risk and ignore it or you know you are certainly doing something and you don't care, that's worse, morally speaking, than if you don't know. And it's worse legally speaking too. A person can usually not be convicted of really serious crimes like murder or larceny for negligent behavior. The behavior must be at least reckless; there must be some subjective awareness of risk or some subjective fault. But some crimes can be based on negligence, as we will see.

You should also note, at this point, that I am here using the words negligence and recklessness in the way that the Model Penal Code defines those terms. Unless otherwise noted, I will continue to use those words, and the words "knowledge" and "purpose," in that model-penal-code sense. But bear in mind that not all courts define these terms this way. So, when reading a case, be very careful to examine and understand how the court is defining its *mens rea* terms — intent, knowledge, recklessness, negligence, willfulness, maliciousness, and so on.

The Model Penal Code says that "ignorance or mistake as to a matter of fact or law" can be a defense if it "negatives the purpose, knowledge, belief, recklessness, or negligence required to establish a material element of the offense." When is ignorance or mistake of fact and law a defense? It is to this issue that we must next turn.

NOTES:

1. *Dennis v. United States*, 341 U.S. 494, 500 (1951).

2. Holmes to Harold Laski, July 14, 1916, in Volume I *of Holmes-Laski Letters*, ed. by M. Wolfe.

3. Model Penal Code, section 2.02 (7).

4. Ira Robbins, "The Ostrich Instruction: Deliberate Ignorance as a Criminal Mens Rea," 81 *Journal of Criminal Law and Criminology* 191 (1990).

5. Model Penal Code, sec. 2.02 (6).

CHAPTER FOUR

Mistake of Fact and Law and Strict Liability

Few topics in criminal jurisprudence have produced more unnecessary confusion than mistake of fact and mistake of law. We are sometimes told, for instance, that mistake of fact is always an excuse and that mistake (or ignorance) of law never is. The reasonableness of the mistake is often regarded as the principal issue; unreasonable ignorance, some say, is not a defense. In reality, none of these generalizations is correct. Only a careful assessment of a variety of types of cases can fully clarify when mistake of fact and mistake of law can exculpate.

1. Mistake of Fact

What does the Model Penal Code mean when it says that ignorance or mistake of fact can negative the material element of an offense? Suppose I am sitting on a park bench. When I get up to leave, I pick up your hat and walk away with it because I mistakenly think it is mine. This is a mistake of fact. Actually it is not necessary to say that I have a mistake of fact defense to a charge of larceny in a case like that. More precisely, I do not have the *mens rea* for larceny at all — intent to steal the property of another person. My ignorance, or mistake of fact, negatives this material element of the offense.

Does it matter if my mistake was not reasonable? In other words, suppose any reasonable person would have noticed that it was not their hat (maybe when I put it on my head, it came way down over my eyes and was obviously too big for me) but I, for some reason, did not realize this. Should I have a defense of mistake of fact? If the crime with which I am charged requires subjective awareness — requires a mental state more culpable than negligence — then it makes sense to say that I *would* have such a defense, even for an unreasonable mistake of fact. Larceny does require subjective awareness. It requires intent to steal, and intent, as we have seen, means either purpose or at least knowledge. Thus, if I could truly say that I did not know it was someone else's hat, and if the jury believed me, I should be acquitted.

But sometimes even an honest and *reasonable* mistake of fact is not a defense. It is not a defense if you would be committing a crime (sometimes even an immoral act) even under the facts as you believed them to be. And mistake of fact is also not a defense if the crime is strict liability.

Consider the following case, about statutory rape:

State v. Stiffler
Court of Appeals of Idaho, 1988

The sole issue is whether an honest and reasonable mistake of fact as to the victim's age is a defense to a charge of statutory rape. We hold it is not . . . .

The underlying premise of rape laws is the lack of a female's consent to an invasion of her bodily privacy. The prohibition against sexual intercourse with a female minor [i.e., *statutory* rape] . . . is an attempt to prevent sexual exploitation of persons deemed legally incapable of giving consent . . . . Stiffler contends that a reasonable mistake of fact as to the victim's age should be a defense because it would disprove any criminal intent to engage in non-consensual sexual activity . . . .

But] criminal intent is not a necessary element of statutory rape. The only elements the state must prove are (1) the conscious performance of sexual intercourse, accomplished with (2) a female under the age of eighteen. Statutory rape is a strict liability offense . . . . A reasonable mistake of fact as to the victim's age is no defense.

Dissent:

Rape is punishable by imprisonment for life. Today the majority holds that this serious felony has been committed when two persons engage in consensual intercourse and the male is reasonably mistaken in an honest belief that the female is eighteen years of age or older . . . . I respectfully disagree.

The jury should decide . . . whether the defendant's alleged mistake was subjectively honest and objectively reasonable. I have faith in the ability of jurors to make this determination.

The majority of states make statutory rape a strict liability crime, but most set the age at sixteen or lower, rather than eighteen as in the *Stiffler* case. The Idaho statute at issue in *Stiffler* is quite like most statutory rape provisions, however, in that it is gender specific: it is not an offense, or at least not an offense of equal severity, for a female to have consensual sexual intercourse with an underage male, but it is an offense for a male to have intercourse with an underage female. Is this sex discrimination? The Supreme Court said no in a case called *Michael M. v. Superior Court* in 1981, citing the state's interest in preventing teenage pregnancies. Some feminists have criticized this decision, as implying that underage women need special protection which underage men do not need.

In non-consensual rape, sometimes called forcible rape, the general rule is that the defendant is not guilty if he reasonably believed that the victim had consented, but he has no defense if his belief about consent was unreasonable. But in an English case, *Director of Public Prosecutions v. Morgan*, in 1976, the House of Lords seemed to take the opposite approach. In the facts of that case, a husband had invited three of his friends, all of whom were members of the Royal Air Force, to his home to have sex with his wife. He falsely told them that his wife would pretend to reject their sexual advances. Believing this, they each had forcible nonconsensual sex with her. In answering a question certified to it for consideration, the House of Lords said that a defendant in such a circumstance should be acquitted even if his mistake of fact was negligent. As Lord Cross of Chelsea put it, a man cannot be said to have committed rape "if he believed that the woman was consenting, . . . whatever his grounds for so believing." But Lord Simon of Glaisdale sharply disagreed, saying that a raped woman "would hardly feel that she was vindicated by being told that her assailant must go unpunished because he believed, quite unreasonably, that she was consenting to sexual intercourse with him."[1]

2. *Mistake of Law*

It is often said that ignorance of the law is not an excuse. Actually, the truth is a bit more complicated. There are two different types of mistake of law — one can be an excuse, the other, generally, cannot be. Let's return to my example of picking up someone else's hat from a bench where I am sitting and walking off with it. If I take it because I made an oral agreement with the owner of the hat and think, wrongly, that this is a binding contract that entitles me to possession of the hat, I am, in a sense, making a mistake of law. I do not understand the legal effect of some collateral matter (our oral agreement) and this causes me not to realize the significance of what I am doing (that I am taking an item of personal property that does not belong to me, one to which I am not entitled). *That sort* of mistake of law can be and usually is a defense. For example, I would not have the *mens rea* for larceny — an intent to steal —if I had this sort of mistake of law. But what if I had another sort of mistake of law? What if I knew that this was not my hat but did not know that taking somebody else's hat was against the law. That sort of mistake of law, that sort of ignorance of the law, would not be an excuse. *That* is what is meant when we say that ignorance of the law is not an excuse.

A number of reasons for this rule have been asserted. But which of them are really persuasive? It is said that everyone is expected to know the law. But why? Not everyone is a lawyer. There are millions of laws, even if we confine ourselves to statutory law. Others say, defendants should not be allowed to pretend that they were ignorant of the law. Such a claim, it is said, would be too difficult for prosecutors to refute. But why? Why should it be any harder to prove that someone was aware of the law than it would be to prove that someone was aware of a risk, and we have seen that most crimes, at least most serious crimes, require such proof.

Probably the best reason we say that ignorance of the law is not an excuse is that a person who does not know that certain things are crimes — that certain behavior is unacceptable — is morally blameworthy and deserves to be punished. The great philosopher Aristotle, who lived and wrote more than two thousand years ago in ancient Greece, explained this. Aristotle invited us to consider a syllogism, or a logical step-by-step argument often used by lawyers: first premise, this piece of personal property (for instance, the hat in the example above) belongs to someone else; second premise, it is wrong to take someone else's property; conclusion: I must not take this item. Aristotle says, if you do not know the first premise — if you do not know this is someone else's hat — you *might* be excused. But if you do not know the second premise — if you do not know it is wrong to take something that does not belong to you, you cannot be excused. You are wicked! Ignorance in *moral* choice, Aristotle said, does not make an act excusable. It is the very *definition* of vice.

Of course, we apply the same principle in our criminal law today, by and large. We would never allow someone accused of murdering small children to come into court and say, "I didn't know it was wrong to murder small children!" And we wouldn't allow ignorance of the law as an excuse in such a case either.

Bear in mind also that not all crimes involve an obviously immoral act. We saw this in the first chapter, where I pointed out that, while some crimes are *mala in se* (bad in themselves), others are *mala prohibita* (bad only because society has voted to prohibit them). For these latter kinds of offenses, there may be situations in which a person is not morally to blame for not knowing the existence of the law, especially when the crime punished involves *inaction* rather than action.

Consider the following hypothetical:

Andy buys and wears a sweat shirt with a pattern of the American flag on the front of it. He is arrested and prosecuted for violating a local ordinance making it a crime to "wear the American flag or an image or likeness thereof as an article of clothing." Assuming the statute is constitutional, does Andy have a defense?

Sometimes courts will allow defendants to say that they acted in reasonable reliance on a statute or judicial decision or an opinion by an administrator of the law, even when that opinion turns out to have been erroneous. In the famous 1960s demonstration case of *Cox v. Louisiana*, the U.S. Supreme Court ruled that protesters could not constitutionally be convicted of the local offense of parading within 100 feet of a courthouse when they did so only after a local police official told them that they could. However, you should know that courts almost *never* allow the defense that my *lawyer* told me it was alright to do it.

3. Strict Liability

Legislatures sometimes provide that conduct *un*accompanied by fault constitutes a crime. They rarely say this expressly. Instead, the statute simply omits any fault-type language. It does not, in other words, use a word like negligently or recklessly or intent or purpose, etc. It just says that whoever does X or causes X result is guilty of a crime. Courts deal with these statutes in different ways. Sometimes the court will say that the statute means what it says: no fault is required for conviction. At other times, the courts read some requirement of fault into the statute. In all the cases, however, the courts are, at least purportedly, trying to ascertain the *legislature's* intent. Did the legislature want to impose liability without fault? A number of factors go into determining the answer to that question. The legislative history of the statute is often considered. The severity of the punishment is also a factor. If the punishment is severe, some form of fault will usually be required. On the other hand, if the harm to the public is very great, the court may conclude that the legislature meant to impose liability without fault. A statute making it a crime to "ship poisonous meat," for example, might well be construed as creating a strict liability offense, in the absence of *mens rea* language. Also, in some cases the court will look at how hard it is for the prosecution to prove fault.

Some of these reasons for holding that the legislature *has* imposed liability without fault help explain why a legislature *would* want to impose liability without fault. Legislatures often impose strict liability when *mens rea* is hard to prove, or when the cost to society of the harm at issue (shipments of poisoned meat, for example) is so great that it outweighs the danger of convicting blameless people (people who *did* ship poisoned meat, but didn't "mean to" do so).

The Supreme Court has spoken of a "presumption that *mens rea* is required" — in other words, a presumption *against* strict liability statutes. And the Court has said that "far more than the simple omission of the appropriate phrase from the statutory definition is necessary to justify dispensing with an intent requirement." On the other hand, the courts are very reluctant to sustain constitutional challenges to strict liability laws. As one scholar has summed up the confusion, the Supreme Court's position seems to be that "*mens rea* is an important requirement, but it is not a constitutional requirement, except sometimes."

Apart from constitutionality, many commentators have questioned the propriety of any strict liability criminal statutes at all. They say that the defendant in such a case is treated unfairly because he is subjected to the stigma of criminal punishment, however mild, without being morally culpable. Others disagree, saying that those who "intentionally engage in certain activities and occupy some peculiar or distinctive position of control [for instance, those who ship meat or package drugs for the public] are to be held [strictly] accountable for the occurrence of certain consequences."

Some alternatives to strict liability have been proposed. We could limit punishment of these offenses to people who were "at fault," but make the penalties higher. This assumes that the reduced likelihood of conviction (it is more difficult to get a conviction if you have to prove fault) will be offset by the increased penalty, and thus the deterrent effect will be the same. Then too, negligence is sometimes proposed as a compromise between requiring subjective fault and imposing strict liability. In other situations, legislatures will impose a first warning rule, whereby the first violation of some regulation which is discovered will result only in a warning but any subsequent violation will lead to criminal liability without fault.

We will see more about strict liability later in the book. For a contemporary application of strict liability issues, consider the following case:

United States v. Flum
Eighth Circuit, 1975

Flum was convicted . . . of attempting to board an aircraft while having about his person a concealed dangerous and deadly weapon, in violation of the Federal Aviation Act . . . . In this appeal, Flum contends . . . there was no evidence tending to establish that he intended to conceal the knives which were discovered during a pre-boarding search of his carry-on luggage and personal belongings. The government . . . contends that the statute does not require proof of such intent . . . .

On July 20, 1973, Flum . . . arrived at the airport [and] . . . proceeded to a security post through which passengers must pass before reaching the departure gate. During the security inspection which followed, guards discovered a switchblade knife . . . and a butcher knife . . . . The butcher knife was found in a suitcase, wrapped in loose clothing. The switchblade knife was found inside a small gray box . . . .

The essential elements of the relevant offense are . . . (1) attempting to board an aircraft (2) while carrying a deadly or dangerous weapon (3) which was concealed on or about the defendant's person. Flum was clearly attempting to board an aircraft, and the deadly and dangerous character of the knives is likewise not disputed. What is disputed is whether the evidence showed beyond reasonable doubt that the weapons were "concealed" within the meaning of the statute.

Flum testified that he had intended to check his bags, in advance of boarding, but lacked time to do so because he had arrived at the airport only five minutes prior to take-off time . . . . If intent to conceal were an essential element of the offense, this would be a compelling argument . . . . The provision of the statute applicable to the instant case makes no reference to intent . . . [There is no indication of] a congressional purpose or policy that intent to conceal must be demonstrated . . . . The statutory penalty, a maximum fine of $1000 or imprisonment for not more than one year or both, makes the offense a misdemeanor and is thus "relatively small." . . . Balanced against the heavy risks to large numbers of passengers . . . we cannot say that the resulting effect [of punishing without proof of intent] is too severe.

Dissent:

The decision of the majority permits imposition of criminal liability upon the housewife who carries scissors in her sewing bag; the fisherman who carries a scaling knife in his tackle box; the professional who carries a letter opener in his briefcase; the

doctor who carries scalpels in his medical bag; and the trades-
man who carries a hammer in his tool kit.

Would Flum be guilty if someone else had placed the knives
in his bag without his awareness or consent?

4. Conclusion

We have now reviewed the two principal elements of all
crimes — the guilty act (*actus reus*) and the guilty mind (*mens rea*).
We have seen that some action (not just an omission) is usually
required, but not always. And we have seen that some subjective
fault (purpose, knowledge, or recklessness, as distinct from negligence or strict liability) is usually required, but not always. Now
we will apply these general principles to specific crimes. The first
crime we will consider is the most serious and infamous of all
crimes — murder.

CHAPTER FIVE

Murder

Consider the following hypothetical case:

Charles Antonius Symingdale is the worst man in New England. He is a professor at Porcupine College of Law who spies on his students, then blackmails them to feed his swollen money bags.

On Friday September 13, 1996, Symingdale telephones Tom Kelly, a pupil in Symingdale's enormous lecture course on "The Law of the Bubonic Plague and Other Comedies." Symingdale tells Kelly that he has the papers to prove that Kelly cheated on his last exam and that he will use them against him if Kelly does not pay him $50,000. Kelly, who knows Symingdale's reputation for bluffing, becomes very angry and shouts obscenities over the phone, but Symingdale just tells him to show up at his office on Monday morning "with the cash or else" and hangs up.

Over the weekend, Kelly talks with his friends and admits to them that he has no idea how to raise the money. He also says he will go to Symingdale's office on Monday to "settle this thing, one way or the other." "I wish he were swimming in a pool of blood," Kelly muses.

On Monday morning, September 16, Kelly enters the school building and walks upstairs to Symingdale's office. He finds the evil professor sitting behind his desk — a desk on which are piled the papers implicating Kelly in the cheating. When Kelly seems surprised by this, Symingdale laughs in his face and orders him to "pay up or be expelled." "You'll never be a bankruptcy lawyer unless you pay me!" Symingdale sneers.

Kelly, who has always dreamed of the exciting life of being a bankruptcy lawyer, is outraged. "That's the last straw!" he explodes. With a look of mad rage, Kelly suddenly picks up the letter opener on Symingdale's desk and jabs it into Symingdale's throat. Blood gushes out of Symingdale's mouth. The professor staggers forward. Kelly then pulls the letter opener out of the throat, which takes some effort since it had become lodged in Symingdale's massive throat muscles, and plunges it into his chest. Symingdale dies seconds later. Kelly flees. Hours later, police catch up with Kelly and charge him.

What crime is Kelly guilty of? Murder? First degree murder? Second degree murder? Manslaughter? Consider these questions in light of this chapter, on intentional murder, and the next chapter, on voluntary manslaughter.

1. Definitions: What is Murder?

An English dramatist living at the time of Shakespeare wrote that "all other crimes only *speak*. Murder *shrieks out.*" Throughout history, there has always been a sense that there is something unique about murder. Of all crimes, it is the most horrible, the most worthy of moral and legal condemnation.

But, what is murder? Some states define murder by statute, but many do not. For example, many state statutes say that murders of this or that type (ex: by torture or with premeditation) are first degree murder and that "all other murders are second degree." To define murder itself, then, we often have to look to the common law definition.

At common law, murder has traditionally been defined as "unlawful killing with malice aforethought." The words "unlawful killing" are not very difficult. This excludes, for example, killing in self-defense. Such an act is justifiable homicide, and therefore not an "unlawful killing." But what about "malice aforethought"?

The difficulty with this term is that it is not interpreted literally at all. It is, rather, what is sometimes described as a technical term of art. A killing *need not* be aforethought, in the sense of premeditated, to be murder. Premeditation and forethought is entirely superfluous to a charge of murder, although it may be necessary to make the murder *first-degree* murder, as we will see. Whether malice is required for murder is a bit more complicated. There is a sense in which all forms of murder have something in common: an indifference to the value of human life. Taken in this way, murder does require malice. But the prosecution does not have to prove any special hatred or maliciousness in most cases of murder. As long as one person kills another, and possessed the requisite *mens rea* at the time of the killing, it is murder.

Two examples will illustrate these points: If you are walking home tonight and happen to have a sharp pair of scissors in your pocket and you unexpectedly come upon someone you do not like and you pull out the scissors and stab him to death, that is murder. The law will not say it is not murder because it is not forethought. In the second example, if a man, watching his terminally ill wife in bed, becomes overcome with grief and puts poison in her drink to end her suffering, thereby killing her, that is murder. The law will not say it is not murder because he did not have malice.

But if "malice aforethought" is not to be taken literally, how do we know whether and when a killing is murder? To answer this question, we need a brief review of the history of the crime of murder, followed by a careful analysis of the types of murder that can exist today.

2. History of Murder

Today, murder is a statutory offense in every American state. But it *began* as a common law crime: in Anglo-American legal history, murder was first defined, and made a crime, by judges.

The development of the law of murder has been a slow process — part judicial, part legislative. It is necessary to have a sense of that process in order to understand the often mysterious terms used by lawyers in present murder cases.

In the early history of English law, any person who caused the death of another person could be subject to criminal punishment. Those who killed by accident or in self-defense were customarily pardoned by the king, but they had to face conviction first. As the great historians of English law Pollock and Maitland put it, in this era, "the man who commits homicide by misadventure or in self-defense deserves *but needs* a pardon."[1]

Gradually, pardons in cases of accident or self-defense became a matter of course. In time, the law developed a distinction between felonious homicides (all of which got the death penalty) and non-felonious homicides (like self-defense and homicide by misadventure, which did not get the death penalty). The word murder was then reserved only for secret killings, where the killer's identity was not known.[2]

The next step was the subdivision of felonious homicides into the now familiar terms murder and manslaughter. Murder came to be called "unlawful killing *with* malice aforethought," and manslaughter was understood as "unlawful killing *without* malice aforethought."

Now, in those early days, "malice aforethought" meant literally what it said. A murderer was a wicked man who had planned and plotted out his crime in advance. In a sense, then, the law recognized only two types of criminal homicide —carefully planned and malicious killings (murder) and sudden impulsive killings resulting from a quarrel (then called *chance medley*, or manslaughter).

Over time, courts and legislatures began to recognize that this distinction was not satisfactory. There were other situations in which a killing should properly be described as murder, and thus merit the most severe punishment. For instance, if someone killed another in a sudden heated quarrel, that was not aforethought or premeditated. And yet, if there were no reasonable explanation or excuse for the sudden heat of passion, the law would not mitigate the crime to manslaughter. Thus, it came to be understood that an unpremeditated but intentional killing without provocation or excuse is also murder.

Then too, people began to see that sometimes even an *unintentional killing* can be murder. In 1600, a shopkeeper became enraged when a man made faces at him from the street. Coming out of the shop, he hit the man so hard that he died. He was indicted and charged with manslaughter, but the judges ultimately held him guilty of murder because, although he did not intend to kill, he did intend serious bodily harm, and there was insufficient cause for the sudden display of passion.[3]

Today there are many circumstances in which an unintended killing can be murder. If I hit you on the head with a brick, intending only to give you a severe concussion, and you die instead, that is murder. If I stand on the roof of a building in a city in the middle of the day and throw heavy beams off the roof and thereby kill someone, that is murder. If I accidentally kill someone while committing a felony, in many states that is murder.

In sum, then, what can we conclude from the history of murder? As LaFave and Scott put it in their contemporary treatise on Criminal Law, the

> . . . moral to be drawn from this short history of murder is that it will not solve modern homicide cases to say simply that murder is the unlawful killing of another with malice aforethought, that manslaughter is the unlawful killing of another without malice aforethought, and that no crime is committed if the killing is lawful. For an understanding of the crime of murder, it is necessary to consider, one by one, the various types of murder which the judges created and which, in general, remain to this day . . . .[4]

What, then, are the types of murder recognized today?

3. Types of Murder

There are at least four types of murder today:

a. **Intent-to-kill murder.** (If A intentionally kills B without justification or excuse and without adequate provocation, it is murder.)

b. **Intent-to-do-grievous-bodily-injury murder.** (If A injures B with the intent to cause B grievous bodily injury but not death, and B dies as a result, A is guilty of murder even though he had no intent to kill. Note that courts differ in how they define "grievous bodily injury" in this context. Some say it means an injury that "imperils life." Others say it can include any injury that "seriously interferes with the victim's health or comfort." For instance, in the *Conley* case, discussed in the previous chapter, if the blow with the wine bottle had resulted in death, some courts might permit a jury to find the defendant guilty of murder, because he intended to interfere seriously with the victim's health and death resulted. Others might say that it is only involuntary manslaughter, unless the ferocity of the blow indicates that the defendant intended to inflict life-threatening injury. The point is: under either approach, you can be guilty of murder even if you did not intend to kill, if you intended to injure very, very seriously.)

c. **Felony Murder**. (We will study this in detail in a subsequent chapter. For now, just be aware that if a state retains the felony murder rule in its strict form, that means that if I kill someone while I am committing a felony, it is automatically murder, whether I killed intentionally or unintentionally or even accidentally.)

d. **Reckless Murder** — sometimes called Depraved Heart Murder. (If A takes a substantial and unjustified risk which results in B's death, A may be guilty of murder if the circumstances show A to have a callous disregard for the value of human life.)

We will see more about unintentional murder — felony murder and reckless murder — in a subsequent chapter. In this chapter, after a review of the elements of all murder, we will focus on intent-to-kill-murder and the dividing line between first- and second-degree murder.

4. *The Elements of Murder*

Most murders have three elements:

a. The *actus reus* of murder can be an act or a culpable omission.

b. The *mens rea* of murder can range from purpose and knowledge (either is sufficient for intent to kill murder) to recklessness (for depraved heart murder). Even negligence, in a sense, can sometimes be the basis for a murder conviction. If I get very drunk and, driving in an extremely reckless manner, kill someone, that can be murder even if I was not aware of the risk at the moment of the crash or when I got behind the wheel of the car. In other words, if the only reason I did not know of the risk is that I was drunk, the court will disregard my drunkenness and ask what risk would I have been aware of had I been sober. This sounds more like negligence (objective standard: what risk would a reasonable person be aware of) than recklessness (subjective standard: what risk was the defendant actually aware of), but it can suffice for a conviction of murder.

Note also that for felony murder, there is no *mens rea* for the murder. In that sense, felony murder is a strict liability crime. More precisely, the *mens rea* for the felony substitutes for the *mens rea* for the murder. If the state proves that I had the necessary intent to commit the felony, it is not necessary for the state to prove that I had any *mens rea* for the killing.

c.) Murder also requires that the defendant **caused the death** of a human being. In other words, both causation and result (death) are required. In old English law, the death had to occur within one year and a day of the attack; otherwise, causation was said not to exist. Today, some states retain this "year and a day rule," but others have long since abolished it.

5. Intent-to-Kill Murder

The most common type of murder is intent-to-kill murder. In general, if A intends to kill B and does kill B, A is guilty of murder, unless there was legal provocation, justification, or excuse for the killing.

What does "intent-to-kill" mean? In Model Penal Code terms, it can mean either killing purposely *or* killing knowingly. It definitely does *not* require any premeditation.

How does the state prove intent to kill? There are some cases where the defendant has actually announced to witnesses that he intends to kill someone, and then does so.[5] But such cases are rare. Often, there are no witnesses. The killer kills in secret, or at least never reveals his intention in spoken words. In such cases, the intent to kill must be inferred from his actions.

We have already seen the rule that a person intends the natural and necessary consequences of his acts. In the context of intent-to-kill murder, that rule has a special application known as the deadly weapons doctrine: if one person **intentionally uses** a deadly weapon against another person (especially against the vital part of the body of another person) and thereby kills him, we can infer that he must have **intended to kill** him. This does *not* mean the killing is necessarily murder. It may be voluntary manslaughter or self defense, for example. But an intent to *kill* is inferred from an intentional *use* of a deadly weapon.

For example, if the jury in the O.J. Simpson criminal case had believed, beyond a reasonable doubt, that Simpson intentionally stabbed his ex-wife with a knife (not intentionally killed, but intentionally stabbed — believed, in other words, that, acting voluntarily, he took a knife in his hand and cut her throat with it), then the jury would have been entitled to infer from this fact that he must have intended to kill her from that stabbing.

What is a "deadly weapon"? In determining whether something is a deadly weapon for purposes of this doctrine, the courts look to what the object intrinsically is, on the one hand, and to how it is used, on the other. In general, a deadly weapon is anything which, from the way it is used, is likely to produce death or serious bodily injury. Obviously, guns, knives, axes, baseball bats, iron bars, rocks, cars, and many other things can qualify as deadly weapons. Even a person's hands or feet have been held to be deadly weapons for the purposes of this doctrine.

Of course, intentional killings with a deadly weapon are not the only ways people intentionally kill each other. In a 1952 case, a wife deliberately nagged her husband into walking through deep snow on a cold day, knowing that he was unaware of his serious heart condition and hoping that the exertion would kill him. It did, and a court later found that, because she was guilty of felonious homicide, the property she inherited from him at this death was in constructive trust for his children by a prior marriage.[6] In other cases, killers have intentionally perjured their victims into the electric chair, or enticed blind people leaning over the edge of tall buildings that it was "all clear ahead," or shouted "your son is dead" to an elderly person known to have a bad heart. In all these types of situations, intent to kill has often been present. If death does result, the killing is often punished as murder.

6. Degrees of Murder

The English judges who created the Anglo-American crime of murder did not divide murder into degrees. That was done by legislatures. Originally, the reason for that division was to reserve the death penalty for the most heinous (first-degree) murders, and limit the punishment for all other murders (second-degree) to imprisonment.

Today, in England and some American states, murder is *not* divided into degrees. This is also the recommendation of the Model Penal Code. But most American states now divide murder into two, occasionally three, degrees. The reason for doing so is still to limit the most severe punishment (death penalty or life in prison) to first-degree murder.

One very common way of distinguishing between first- and second-degree murder is by saying that "willful, premeditated, and deliberate murder" is murder of the first degree, and all other murder is of the second degree. What is "willful, premeditated, and deliberate murder"?

7. Willful, Premeditated, And Deliberate Murder

Cardozo once said that "the phrase 'willful, premeditated, and deliberate' is so obscure that no jury hearing it . . . can fairly be expected to assimilate and understand it." Courts sometimes use the terms interchangeably. At other times, they insist that each of the three words has a separate meaning. But juries are given few if any guidelines to determine how to assess what the meanings are or how to apply them in a case.

One thing we can say for certain about all three of these words — willful, premeditated, and deliberate. All three refer to *subjective* fault. All three, in other words, ask us to look into the defendant's own mind, to determine what he was thinking and when. Mistake of fact, then, would be a defense that would preclude a finding of a willful, premeditated, and deliberate murder. So too, in most states, would voluntarily induced intoxication, provided it was strong enough to make it impossible for the person to have any fixed intent or purpose to kill.

The word *willful* seems to be synonymous with *intentional*. It is not always clear, however, whether we are speaking about an intent to kill or an intent to shoot (or stab, etc.). Also, while killing someone with intent to do grievous bodily harm can be murder, it is not always clear whether such a killing would be willful or whether a "specific intent to *kill*" is required.

Premeditated seems to mean "thought about beforehand." But how long beforehand? Some courts say, "no time is too short for premeditation." For instance, in *Commonwealth v. Carrol*, the Pennsylvania Supreme Court ruled that the defendant could have premeditated the murder of his wife in the few seconds it took him to reach for the gun lying next to their bed and fire it into his sleeping wife's head. Under this approach, premeditation is largely synonymous with intent to kill.

For another example of this approach, consider the following:

State v. Schrader
Supreme Court of Appeals, West Virginia, 1982

The appellant . . . was found guilty of murder in the first degree . . . and sentenced to life imprisonment. He appeals.

[Appellant went to a gun shop to trade souvenirs. An argument broke out between appellant and the victim about the authenticity of a German sword. Appellant stabbed the victim 51 times with a hunting knife and he died. The trial judge instructed the jury that "to constitute a willful, deliberate, and premeditated killing, it is not necessary that the intention to kill should exist for any set length of time prior to the actual killing."]

Appellant contends that such an instruction takes the "pre" out of premeditation . . . . We disagree.

The appellant assumes that premeditation as used in a murder statute has the same meaning as that found in a dictionary. [But] . . . the mental process necessary to constitute 'willful, deliberate, and premeditated' murder can be accomplished . . . in the proverbial 'twinkling of an eye.'

[The court quotes a 1795 case: "Let it be supposed that a man, without uttering a word, should strike another on the head with an axe, it must . . . be deemed a premeditated violence."]

Conviction affirmed.

If no time is too short for premeditation, even a large amount of time does not prove there was premeditation if the defendant did not actually premeditate. And courts will often look at the defendant's *capacity* to premeditate. In *People v. Caruso* (1927), an illiterate, foreign-born man unreasonably believed that a doctor's malpractice had caused his child's death and that the doctor laughed when the child died. Outraged, he choked and stabbed the doctor to death. An appellate court *reversed* his conviction for first degree murder because there was only evidence of *time* and not of *capacity* to premeditate.

This emphasis on capacity brings us to the third word in our trilogy: **deliberate**. As a verb, to deliberate means to consider, to think carefully. As an adjective, deliberate usually means careful, unhurried, cautious. As a way of describing murder, it is difficult to distinguish between the terms "deliberate" and "premeditated." One recent attempt to distinguish them puts the matter this way:

> It has been suggested that for premeditation, the killer asks himself the question, " Shall I kill him?" The intent to kill aspect of the crime is found in the answer, "yes, I shall." The deliberation part of the crime requires a thought like, "Wait, what about the consequences? Well, I'll do it anyway."[7]

Similarly, *Wharton's Criminal Law* defines deliberation as "the process of carefully weighing the alternatives of killing or not killing." One thinks of Shakespeare's Macbeth, contemplating his planned killing of the king: "Is this a dagger that I see before me?" Other authorities insist that "it is not possible for a person to deliberate unless she premeditates. Nonetheless, it is possible to premeditate without possessing the calmness and depth of thought characteristic of 'deliberation.'"[8]

Many courts emphasize that a person cannot deliberate if he or she does not possess *a cool mind capable of reflection*. But if there was cool, calm reflection when the intent to kill was formed, it doesn't make any difference if the defendant was in a hot passion when he executed the plan. If John Wilkes Booth carefully planned to kill President Lincoln and then got drunk and executed his plan in a frenzied rage, the court might well say that this was still a premeditated, willful, and deliberate murder. On the other hand, if the defendant was in a passion when he formed the intent, there can still be deliberate murder if the defendant executes the intent after the passion subsides.

In short, while some courts continue to adhere to the "no time is too short" approach to premeditation, many others require that "the interval between initial thought and ultimate actions should be long enough to afford a reasonable man time to subject the nature of his response to a 'second look.'" A famous example of this approach is *People v. Anderson*, where the California Supreme Court ruled that a man who killed a 10-year-old girl by stabbing her wildly over 60 times was not guilty of premeditated murder because there was no evidence that the killing was the result of pre-existing reflection and actual deliberation.

Are premeditated killings worse? Consider the following case:

Midgett v. State
Supreme Court of Arkansas, 1987
Newbern, Justice, announced the opinion of the court.

This child abuse case resulted in the appellant's conviction of first degree murder . . . . We hold that there was no evidence of the . . . "premeditated and deliberate purpose . . ." required for conviction of first degree murder . . . .

The appellant is six feet two inches tall and weighs 300 pounds. His son, Ronnie Midgett, Jr., was eight years old and weighed between thirty-eight and forty-five pounds.

The evidence showed that Ronnie had been abused by brutal beatings over a substantial period of time . . . . His mother, the wife of the appellant, was not living in the home . . . .

Ronnie's sister . . . testified that on the Saturday preceeding the Wednesday of Ronnie Jr.'s death their father, the appellant, was drinking whiskey (two to three quarts that day) and beating on Ronnie Jr . . . . On direct examination, she said that . . . she had seen the appellant choke him for no particular reason on Sunday night after she and Ronnie Jr. returned from church . . . .

On the Wednesday Ronnie Jr. died, the appellant appeared at a hospital carrying the body. An autopsy . . . showed Ronnie was very poorly nourished . . . . There were recently caused bruises [all over the body, including] recent as well as older rib fractures.

The conclusion of the medical examiner . . . was that Ronnie died as the result of intra-abdominal hemorrhage caused by a blunt force trauma consistent with having been delivered by a human fist.

The appellant argues that, in spite of all this evidence of child abuse, there is no evidence that he killed Ronnie Jr. having premeditated and deliberated causing his death. We must agree.

The evidence in this case supports only the conclusion that the appellant intended, not to kill his son, but to further abuse him, or that his intent, if it was to kill the child, was developed in a drunken, heated rage while disciplining the child. Neither of these supports a finding of premeditation or deliberation.

Hickman, dissenting:

. . . the degree of murder committed is for the jury to decide — not us . . . . The state proved Midgett starved the boy, choked him, and struck him several times in the stomach and back. The jury could easily conclude that such repeated treatment was intended to kill the child . . . .

I cannot fathom how this father could have done what he did; but it is not my place to sit in judgment of his mental state, nor allow my human feelings to color my judgment . . . [but] if one does certain acts and the result is murder, one must pay.

How would this case have been decided under the *Carrol* and *Anderson* approaches to premeditation? How should it be decided?

State v. Forrest
Supreme Court of North Carolina, 1987

Defendant was convicted of the first degree murder of his father . . . [and] sentenced . . . to life imprisonment. [He appeals.]

On 22 December 1985, defendant . . . admitted his critically ill father to [the hospital]. Defendant's father . . . was suffering from numerous serious ailments, including severe heart disease . . . . His medical condition was determined to be untreatable and terminal . . . .

On 24 December 1985, defendant went to the hospital to visit his ailing father. No other family members were present . . . . The nurse's assistant noticed that defendant was sniffling as though crying and that he kept his hand in his pocket during their conversation. She subsequently went to get the nurse . . . .

[When the nurse and assistant returned, defendant told the nurse that his father was dying. The nurse tried to comfort him, saying that he may be getting better.] Defendant, very upset, responded, "Go to hell. I've been taking care of him for years. I'll take care of him." Defendant was then left alone in the room with his father.

Alone at his father's bedside, defendant began to cry and to tell his father how much he loved him. His father began to cough, emitting a gurgling and rattling noise. Extremely upset, defendant pulled a small pistol from his pants pocket, put it to his father's temple, and fired. He subsequently fired three more times and walked into the hospital corridor, dropping the gun to the floor just outside his father's room.

Following the shooting, defendant, who was crying and upset, neither ran nor threatened anyone. Moreover, he never denied shooting his father and talked openly with law enforcement officials . . . . "He's out of his suffering . . . . I know the doctors couldn't do it, but I could . . . . I promised my dad I wouldn't let him suffer."

Though defendant's father had been near death as a result of his medical condition, the exact cause of the deceased's death was determined to be the four point-blank bullet wounds to the head. Defendant's weapon was a single-action .22 caliber five-shot revolver. The weapon, which had to be cocked each time it was fired, contained four empty shells and one live round . . . .

The jury found defendant guilty of first-degree murder.

[He appeals, contending that] there was insufficient evidence of premeditation and deliberation . . . . We do not agree. First-degree murder is the intentional and unlawful killing of a human being with malice and with premeditation and deliberation . . . . Among other circumstances to be considered in determining whether a killing was with premeditation and deliberation are: (1) want of provocation on the part of the deceased; (2) the conduct and statements of the defendant before and after the killing . . . .

[Here] the seriously ill deceased did nothing to provoke defendant's action. Moreover, the deceased was lying helpless in a hospital bed when defendant shot him four separate times. In addition, defendant's revolver . . . had to be cocked each time before it could be fired. Interestingly, although defendant testified that he always carried the gun in his job as truck driver, he was not working on the day in question but carried the gun to the hospital nonetheless.

Most persuasive of all . . . are defendant's own statements following the incident . . . . Defendant stated that he had thought about putting his father out of his misery because he knew he was suffering. [On these facts, the jury could reasonably find first-degree murder.]

Do the *Midgett* and *Forrest* cases show that the drafters of the Model Penal Code were right when they said that the idea "that the person who plans ahead is worse than the person who kills on sudden impulse . . . does not survive analysis"?

8. Alternatives to Premeditation

Some states do not use premeditation or deliberation to

distinguish first degree murder. Still others do use these terms, but also specify that a killing can be first degree murder even without premeditation or deliberation if it was perpetrated in various particularly bad ways.

For example, in **Massachusetts**, first degree murder is:

1) murder committed with **deliberately premeditated malice aforethought** (the Massachusetts courts have held that no set time is required — only the time needed to form a clear intent to kill. The deadly weapons doctrine is used to infer intent to kill);

2) murder committed in the course of a crime punishable by death or life imprisonment (including the felonies of rape, robbery, kidnapping for extortion of money, armed burglary, and possession of a machine gun) (**first-degree felony murder**);

3) murder committed with **extreme atrocity and cruelty**.

What is a murder committed with "extreme atrocity and cruelty"? Some states are more specific in their statutes. They provide that killing "by torture, lying in wait, or poison" is murder in the first degree.

There is no doubt that many murders by such means are extremely gruesome, and, if the atrocity of the killing should make the difference between first- and second-degree murder, they would seem to qualify for the higher grade of the crime. One California case from the 1950s comes to mind. In *People v. Martinez*, the defendant soaked his wife in gasoline and lit a match. She burned very slowly, dying three days later.

On the other hand, there are serious problems with using the manner of killing to distinguish degrees of murder. If the legislature says that murder "by torture" is first degree murder, the court will not be satisfied with such a verdict unless it is clear that the torture *caused* the death. For instance, in one case, the defendant burned his victim with a flaming torch but did not kill her. He then raped and strangled her. The court held he was not guilty of first-degree murder by torture because the burning did not cause the death. The strangulation killed her, and strangulation is not torture.

Similar problems plague courts dealing with statutes that speak of "lying in wait" murder. Lying in wait is usually defined to mean watching and waiting in a concealed position, with intent to kill or do serious bodily injury. But courts have held that it is not lying in wait to stand outside a building with a gun in hand, anticipating the victim, or to sit in a parked car across the street from the victim's store before shooting him, or to follow the victim home on the street. Lying in wait means precisely what it says: *hiding* in a very concealed place, and then jumping out and killing. Are such killings necessarily worse?

The most significant problems arise when legislatures say that killing by *poison* is first degree murder. Courts usually say that this means the defendant must have intended to *kill* by the poison. For example, if defendant put poison in the victim's coffee, hoping to drug him and put him to sleep so he would not resist when defendant robbed him, and victim died from the poison, many courts would say that this is not first degree murder by poison because there was no *intent to kill by poison.*

On the other hand, some courts have held that, when the legislature says that murder by poison is first degree murder, then premeditation, deliberation, and even intent to kill are totally irrelevant. The North Carolina Supreme Court so held in the recent case of *State v. Johnson.* In that case, the defendant poisoned his five-year-old daughter by pretending to give her a teaspoon of medicine but in fact giving her a teaspoon of bug poison. The trial judge refused to instruct the jury that a finding of first degree murder requires proof of an intent to kill. Convicted of first degree murder, which the legislature had defined as murder "by means of poison, lying in wait, imprisonment, starving, torture, or by any other kind of willful, deliberate, and premeditated killing," the defendant appealed. The state's highest court affirmed, saying that intent to kill was irrelevant. As long as the defendant intended to administer the poison, acted with malice, and the victim died from the poisoning, there is first degree murder, regardless of premeditation or intent to kill.

This decision seems to mean that, if the defendant had killed his daughter by shooting her or stabbing her or even decapitating her with one sudden blow, he could not be guilty of first degree murder unless the state proved premeditation and intent to kill, but that because he killed her with poison, he is automatically guilty of first degree murder. And it is not impossible to kill by poison without intent to kill. Suppose a man puts insecticide in his wife's drink hoping to make her sick so she will not be able to accompany him to a dance where he hopes to meet his girlfriend. The wife dies from the insecticide. If murder by poison is automatically first degree murder, this would be first degree murder without proof of premeditation or intent to kill. But if he had stabbed her in the neck, hoping the wound would keep her in bed so he could go to the dance, this might well not be first degree murder unless there was proof that he intended to kill her and thought about it beforehand.

Speaking of stabbing, one also wonders whether death by poison — or by torture, for that matter — is necessarily always the worst. The great murder novelist Agatha Christie was apparently of the view that murder with a knife was the worst. In *The Plymouth Express*, she has her hero, Hercule Poirot, say that:

> Of all forms of killing, I wonder if to kill by a knife is not the worst of all. To feel the victim's breath upon one's face. To feel the scrape of the knife against the ribs.

In sum, it is worth asking whether any of the definitions of first degree murder really helps us distinguish the more brutal murders, those most worthy of the highest punishment.

We will return to murder in subsequent chapters, when we take up unintentional murder — reckless murder and felony murder. Now, we need to interrupt our study of murder and consider another form of intentional killing. Under what circumstances is a killing that would otherwise be murder considered only voluntary manslaughter?

NOTES

1. Sir Frederick Pollock and Frederic William Maitland, *History of English Law Before The Time of Edward I*, 2 Vols. (2nd Edit. 1898, reissued 1968), Vol II, p. 479.

2. J. H. Baker, *An Introduction to English Legal History*, 2nd Edition (London: Butterworths, 1979), p. 429.

3. *Watts v. Brains* (1600) Cro Eliz 778, Noy 171, Brit Lib MS Add. 25203, f.216v.

4. Wayne LaFave and Austin Scott, Jr., *Criminal Law*, 2nd Edition (St. Paul: West Publishing Co., 1986), p. 606.

5. See, for example, *State v. Jensen*, 120 Utah 531, 236 P.2d 445 (1951), where the court says that "there could hardly be more direct or certain evidence of the defendant's intent than for him to declare — before, during, and after the attack — his intention to kill." Quoted in LaFave and Scott, p. 613, n.11.

6. *Vesey v. Vesey,* 237 Minn. 295, 54 N.W. 2nd 385 (1952).

7. LaFave and Scott, *Criminal Law,* 2nd ed., p. 643.

8. See Joshua Dressler, *Understanding Criminal Law* (Bender: 1987/1995), p. 459.

CHAPTER SIX

Voluntary Manslaughter

It is, of course, useless to define manslaughter as "unlawful killing *without* malice aforethought," although many states continue to do so. More practically, manslaughter can be seen as a kind of halfway house between murder, on the one hand, and justifiable homicide on the other. Manslaughter is a very serious crime, but not as serious as murder. It thus includes forms of criminal homicides which are not "serious" enough to be classed as murder.

Like murder, manslaughter was originally a common law crime, created and defined by judges in England. In time, those judges came to distinguish between two kinds of manslaughter — **voluntary** manslaughter, or killing in a sudden heat of passion, and **involuntary** manslaughter. Involuntary manslaughter, in turn, has come to be classified into two types — or killing as the result of an unlawful act (e.g., assault), sometimes called "unlawful act manslaughter," and killing as the result of doing a lawful act (e.g., driving a car) in an unlawful way (e.g., negligently), sometimes called "criminal negligence manslaughter" or "reckless manslaughter." Today, some states have abolished this distinction by statute, replacing it with degrees of manslaughter, each punished by different terms of imprisonment.

Many states, however, do retain the voluntary/involuntary manslaughter dichotomy, and they usually provide a more severe penalty for voluntary manslaughter than for involuntary. In this chapter, I will first review the common law approach to voluntary manslaughter, which focuses on provocation. Then I will discuss the model penal code approach, which does not use the terms voluntary and involuntary for manslaughter, but which does specify that one of the ways in which a killing can be manslaughter is by "extreme emotional disturbance" — a condition comparable to, but by no means the same as, the common law "heat of passion."

1. Rationale of Voluntary Manslaughter

Re-read carefully the hypothetical about Professor Symingdale at the start of the previous chapter. We have already seen that, *if* the killing there is murder, it could be first or second-degree murder, depending on how the court defines premeditation. But is it murder at all?

As discussed in the previous chapter, an intentional killing can, of course, be murder. But it is not murder if it was the result of mitigating circumstances. By mitigating, we do not mean circumstances that make it not a crime at all — like self-defense. Rather, we mean circumstances that reduce the crime (mitigate it) to a lower degree of homicide. If, when the defendant killed, he was in a state of passion produced by legally sufficient provocation, the law will say the killing was not murder, but voluntary manslaughter.

But what is the rationale of this mitigation doctrine? As Joshua Dressler puts it in his *Understanding Criminal Law*, "why should people who become angry and kill a human being when provoked escape society's most severe punishment"?[1] Why should the mitigating plea of voluntary manslaughter exist at all? If a person steals while in a state of extreme passion, or rapes while in a state of extreme passion, we do not allow them to mitigate their crime from larceny or rape to "voluntary larceny" or "voluntary rape." Indeed, there is no such thing as voluntary larceny or voluntary rape. Why should there be such a thing as "voluntary manslaughter." Why are *killings* done in passion sometimes punished less?

Neither courts nor commentators have produced a satisfactory explanation of this doctrine. The positivist legal philosopher John Austin stated the puzzle well: is the reason for the mitigating plea that the defendant, being in an impulsive or passionate state, is less responsible for his act, or is it that, his victim "having done . . . such an injury, [he] was entitled to retaliate"?[2] If the former, then a plea of voluntary manslaughter is properly understood as a species of **excuse**. If the latter, it is properly understood as a species of **justification**.

What is meant here by justification and excuse? We will examine these terms in more detail later in the book when we take up the subject of defenses. But a word of explanation is necessary now. Justification means that society is, in a sense, expressing its approval of the defendant's conduct. Any reasonable person would (perhaps should) have acted as he did. Self-defense is a justification defense. Any reasonable person kills when doing so is necessary to save himself from one who poses an immediate threat to his life. Excuse, on the other hand, focuses on the defendant himself, not on the act. An excuse defense means that the act itself is blameworthy, but the actor is not. Insanity is an excuse defense. When an insane person kills, we do not say that the killing is justifiable or reasonable. We say that this defendant is not responsible for the act because he was insane.

There are two senses in which a plea of voluntary manslaughter is often not a "defense" at all. First, it is certainly not a "complete defense" in the way that self-defense or insanity is. If you are charged with murder and you acted in self-defense, that is a complete defense: you are not guilty of *any* crime. But, if you plead voluntary manslaughter, you are not asserting that you committed no crime. Rather, you claim that the crime should be reduced (mitigated) from murder to voluntary manslaughter.

A plea of voluntary manslaughter is often not an "affirmative defense." An affirmative defense is generally one for which the defense has the burden of persuading the jury. But it may not be up to the defense to persuade the jury that the defendant was in a heat of passion. If the defendant raises the issue of provocation or heat of passion, the prosecution may have the burden of persuading the jury that the crime should not be mitigated in that way.

Looked at in a broader way, voluntary manslaughter is a defense. It is a way that a person, charged with murder, can try to avoid the law's most severe sanction. But is it analogous to a justification defense or an excuse defense? Do we have this defense because the defendant's conduct was justified (because the victim, in a sense, deserved what he got)? Or do we have it because the defendant's conduct was excused (because the defendant was not fully responsible for what he was doing)?

Courts and commentators have rationalized voluntary manslaughter using both approaches, and neither fully explains this "defense." For instance, in support of the view that voluntary manslaughter is a species of justification, one can point to the fact that, at common law, lawful conduct, no matter how provocative, is generally never considered sufficient provocation to reduce murder to manslaughter. Insulting words, however enraging, have often been held not sufficient provocation. Then too, while the classic situation of voluntary manslaughter is that of a husband returning home to find his wife in bed with her lover, courts following the strict common law view have held that it is murder if a man returns home to find his lover, to whom he is not married, in bed with someone else. Is this because adultery is a form of injustice which *deserves* killing, while mere sexual unfaithfulness of one's unmarried partner does not? Courts in the old days said things like that. Some went so far as to suggest that a husband who kills his wife or her lover when caught in the act should only be guilty of voluntary manslaughter, not murder, because adultery is the "highest invasion of his property."[3]

Yet another example illustrating the justification rationale of voluntary manslaughter is the **misdirected retaliation** doctrine. Under this doctrine, a subspecies of the common law approach to provocation, the mitigating plea of voluntary manslaughter is only applicable when it is the person who gets killed who provoked the killing. For instance, suppose the defendant's wife suddenly tells him that her two-month old baby is not his. A shouting match between the married couple ensues. The defendant, in a violent rage, takes the baby out of the house and smothers it.[4] Is this murder or voluntary manslaughter? If the doctrine of misdirected retaliation applies, it is murder, because the defendant took his rage out on the "wrong" person.

As another example, consider a person who, on witnessing his child get run over by a truck, lashes out at an innocent bystander, killing him with a knife to the chest in a fit of furious rage and grief. Looked at from the point of view of justification, we *might* be able to see why this killing is murder, but killing of the person who drove the truck would only be voluntary manslaughter. But looked at from the point of view of excuse, the distinction makes no sense. The defendant was in an emotionally passionate state — a state aroused by an act (the killing of his child before his very eyes) which would be likely to arouse such a passion in a person of reasonable temper. Why is that passion less relevant if he kills an "innocent" bystander than if he kills the truck driver? In either case, the defendant's act may be said to be partly excusable, because he wasn't in full control of himself.

Looking at voluntary manslaughter as excuse poses problems too. What does it mean to say that the defendant wasn't in "full control of himself"? Does it mean that he was so "dethroned of reason" that he momentarily lacked the intent to kill? Probably not. He *did* intend to kill the bystander. He pulled out a knife and plunged it into his chest. Does it mean that he was temporarily insane? In a way, perhaps, but not in the way the law defines insanity. After all, then why should it be a crime in any sense? Does it mean he was acting involuntarily? But surely not involuntarily in the way used in the *actus reus* doctrine. He was not sleepwalking or having a muscle spasm. In the end, then, *if* voluntary manslaughter is a species of excuse, it can be explained only because, in general, the law considers that a person who is in a state of passion when he kills — a state of passion aroused by an event which would be likely to arouse such passion in any reasonable person — is less morally and legally blameworthy than one who kills in "cold blood."

2. Elements of Common Law Voluntary Manslaughter

Under the common law, for murder to be reduced to voluntary manslaughter, four things must be true:

a. there was legally sufficient **provocation**;

b. the defendant was **actually provoked** by this;

c. a **reasonable man** would **not** have had time to **cool off** between the provocation and the killing;

d. the **defendant** did **not** in fact **cool off.**

a. **Legally Sufficient Provocation**

Under English homicide law, the provocation must be "enough to make a reasonable man do as he did."[5] But American courts have correctly seen the fallacy in this way of putting it. A reasonable man never kills in a heat of passion. And if any reasonable man would have done as the defendant did, why is the defendant guilty of any crime at all?

Rather, it is more precise to say that the provocation must be sufficient to cause any reasonable person to lose his self-control, or be *tempted* to rash or violent action. What is sufficient to do that?

Consider the following hypotheticals. In which, if any, can the defendant plead voluntary manslaughter?

1) Thadeus Small slaps Sherlock Holmes in the face. Sherlock then pushes Thadeus into a wall and hits him hard in the leg with his cane. Thadeus pulls out a knife and stabs Sherlock to death.

2) During a friendly boxing match, Ernie hits Bob below the belt. Enraged, Bob chokes Ernie to death.

3) Determined to teach Bill Archer a lesson, Lucius walks up to Bill and threatens to beat him up. Terrified, Bill pulls out a gun and shoots Lucius to death.

4) Police Officer Jones breaks into Tommy Tomkins' house illegally without a warrant and arrests him for a murder Tommy did not commit. Struggling with the officer, Tommy pushes him into the highway, where a truck hits and kills him.

5) Tom and Bruce are walking home when Billy hits Tom in the face with a wine bottle. Enraged, Bruce picks up a sharp piece of glass from the broken bottle and plunges it into Billy's throat, killing him.

6) Upon hearing verdict of "Not Guilty," father of victim killed by O.J. Simpson pulls out a gun and shoots O.J. and the judge, killing both instantly.

b. **Was the defendant, in fact, provoked?**

Even if there was legally sufficient provocation, the defendant cannot plead voluntary manslaughter if he was not, in fact, provoked by it — in other words, if he, in fact, killed in cold blood.

Consider the following hypothetical:

Roger Thornycroft returns one night to find his wife in bed with another man. Surprised but still thinking calmly, he walks over to the window, closes the curtains, removes a gun from his desk drawer, and then shoots his wife and her lover in the head.

c. **Would a reasonable person have had time to cool off?**

If a reasonable person would have cooled off in the time between the provocation and the killing, the defendant cannot plead voluntary manslaughter even if he did not cool off in that time. But, if some event rekindles the earlier passion, the defendant can plead voluntary manslaughter.

Consider the following, based on real cases:

1) A commits sodomy on B while B is unconscious. The next day, A spreads the news that B has engaged in sodomy, angering B. Two weeks after the sodomy incident, when B is ridiculed in public for the sodomy act, B, furious, kills A. Is B guilty of first degree murder? Second degree murder? Voluntary manslaughter?

2) A finds out that B has had sex with his 15-year-old daughter. He goes to B's house and argues with him. Two weeks later, B shows up at A's house and says, "I'll do as I please with that whore!" A flies into a rage and chokes B to death.

d. **Did the defendant, in fact, cool off?**

Even if the defendant was provoked, by a legally sufficient provocation, and even if a reasonable person would not have cooled off, courts following the strict common law view will say that the defendant is not entitled to a voluntary manslaughter instruction if the defendant did, in fact, cool off.

In sum, under the common law, if I intentionally kill you under circumstances which would tempt a reasonable person to lose control and act from passion rather than judgment, I am only guilty of voluntary manslaughter, provided that I was actually provoked, that a reasonable person would not have cooled off, and that I had not cooled off. But what if a defendant cannot successfully assert all four of the required claims for voluntary manslaughter? Suppose, for example, a defendant killed in a heat

of passion, but a reasonable person would not have been provoked in the first place (there was no legally sufficient provocation) or a reasonable person would have cooled off. What crime
is the defendant guilty of? Most courts would say *second*-degree
murder, because, although the defendant intended to kill, there
was no coolness of mind and/or deliberation which traditionally
characterizes first-degree murder. Suppose, on the other hand,
one kills under circumstances which would enrage a reasonable
person and it is clear that a reasonable person would not have
cooled off, but this defendant was acting in cold blood because he
was not provoked to violent temper in the first place or had
cooled off. Then, most courts would say the defendant is guilty of
first-degree murder — he killed deliberately, in cold blood, even
though a reasonable person might have been in an uncontrollable
rage.

3. Who Decides Provocation

Traditionally, the question of whether there was sufficient
provocation and whether a reasonable person would have cooled
off were questions of law, decided by the judge. And, as we have
seen, all the factors that went into voluntary manslaughter were
interpreted according to rigid rules — words are not enough, no
misdirected retaliation, and so on. More recently, however, state
legislatures and courts have adopted a less rigid view of this
"defense" and have put the issue of provocation to the jury.

In keeping with this trend away from the fixed categories of
the past is the model-penal-code approach, to which we now
turn.

4. The Model Penal Code Approach

Under the code, "criminal homicide constitutes manslaughter when it is committed recklessly or . . . under the influence of
extreme mental or emotional disturbance for which there is
reasonable explanation or excuse." This "extreme emotional
disturbance" defense is the code's counterpart of the common
law's voluntary manslaughter. But the code expands on the heat-
of-passion "defense" in several important ways. First, it does not

require provocation. Instead, it speaks only of "emotional disturbance." Second, there is no requirement of suddenness; a long-
smoldering resentment will sometimes be sufficient. Third, the
drafters of the code apparently intended to do away with some of
the rigid common law rules — like the rule against misdirected
retaliation.

But as the case of *People v. Casassa* makes clear, the model-
penal-code approach is also *similar* to the common law in that it
is partly objective: it does require that there be a "reasonable
explanation or excuse for the defendant's behavior." Still, the
Code also provides that the reasonableness of that behavior is to
be determined "from the viewpoint of a person in the actor's
situation under the circumstances as he believes them to be."
What is meant by "situation"? What personal qualities of the
accused can be taken into account?

Consider the following hypotheticals:

1) Muhammed, a native of an Islamic country residing in
the United States, is outraged when he sees a young couple
kissing in the subway in Boston. In his culture, such public
displays of emotion are extremely scandalous and shocking.
Infuriated, he beats the couple to death with his umbrella. Can he
plead voluntary manslaughter in mitigation? Is the standard that
of a reasonable man, or that of a reasonable man of Islamic
culture?

2) Natalie returns home to find her husband kissing a
strange woman in her living room. Flying into a rage, she picks up
a book and hits him over the head, killing him. Should the
standard be that of the "reasonable man"? The "reasonable
woman"? The reasonable "person"? Consider the following data:
a recent study showed that 87% of those arrested for homicide in
the United States were men. As some commentators have put it,
"homicide is overwhelmingly a male act . . . . Women rarely
kill."[6] How would this influence your decision as to which
standard to apply?

5. Conclusion

We have now seen two crimes that can result from an intentional killing — murder (of the first- or second-degree) and

voluntary manslaughter. But what of unintentional killings?

Under what circumstances can a defendant be guilty of a serious crime like manslaughter when he did not know of the risk he was posing to others? Under what circumstances can a defendant be guilty of murder when he did not intend to kill?

NOTES

1. Joshua Dressler, *Understanding Criminal Law* (New York: Matthew Bender, 1987/1995), p. 476. Of course, as Dressler acknowledges, anger is not the only intense emotion that can give rise to a voluntary manslaughter situation. Killings committed as the result of extreme fear or desperation have sometimes been classed as voluntary manslaughter. Indeed, virtually any "violent, intense, high-wrought, or enthusiastic emotion" can suffice for voluntary manslaughter. A desperate desire for revenge, for example for the Waco bombing, however, will not suffice.

2. *Ibid.* p. 474.

3. The "male domination" characteristic of the law of voluntary manslaughter has been well documented.

4. See *Thibodeaux v. State,* Court of Appeals of Texas, 1987, as cited in Dressler, *Cases and Materials on Criminal Law* (St. Paul: West, 1994), pp. 223-4.

5. Honicide Act, 1957, 5 & 6 Eliz. 2, c.11, sec. 3, cited in Dressler, *Understanding Criminal Law.*

6. See Laurie Taylor, Comment: "Provoked Reason in Men and Women: Heat-Of-Passion Manslaughter and Imperfect Self-Defense," 33 UCLA L.Rev. 1679, 1679-81 (1986).

Reckless Murder and Involuntary Manslaughter

The following hypothetical case is relevant to this chapter, on unintentional homicide, as well as to the next two chapters, on felony murder and group crimes respectively.

On Tuesday June 10, 1997, a mysterious and ominous notice appears in *The New England Gazette*: "A crime will take place tomorrow at noon at the Puffendorf School of Law (PSL)." There is no explanation, and readers of the paper assume it is "some sort of silly hoax."

Bill Caruthers and Mary Wilkins, the two PSL students who put the ad in the paper as a joke, decide to play a trick on first year law student Thadeus Jones. They tell Jones that they are going to pretend to rob the school at noon on Wednesday the 11th, wearing masks and carrying guns loaded with blanks. "It's a big joke," they say. "We'll run in, wave our guns like Jesse James, demand some cash, then run out, shooting our blanks in the air. It'll be wild!," Caruthers says. Jones agrees to join them.

Just before noon on Wednesday the 11th, all three students go to the school building together for their "fun adventure." On the way to the school, Caruthers whispers to Wilkins that he has actually loaded Jones's gun with *real bullets*. "I can't wait to see Jones's reaction when he fires that thing in the air — and it puts a hole in the ceiling!," Caruthers laughs. They agree not to tell Jones about this little "surprise."

All three students arrive at the school, wearing their masks, at precisely noon. They burst in the front door of the administration office, yelling, "Stick-em up! Your money or your life!" A secretary screams and, believing it to be a real hold up, reaches in the desk for some money to hand over. Ignoring her, Caruthers and Wilkins turn around and fire their blanks in the air as they head for the door. Jones takes some of the money from the secretary (all part of the joke, he thinks; he plans to return it a few minutes later) and turns to leave.

Just at that moment, a student in Matthew Pauley's criminal law class, Jonathan Prendergast, walks into the administration office, a little bleary-eyed after yet another boring Pauley lecture. "What's going on here?," he asks. Jones looks at Prendergast, smiles, and says. "It's just a joke!" Then Jones points his gun directly at Prendergast's head and pulls the trigger.

The gun goes off, killing Prendergast instantly. Panicking, Caruthers and Wilkins grab Jones and together they run out the door and jump into Wilkins' car, which is parked nearby. With Wilkins driving, they speed toward Providence, where they hope to escape by flying to Antarctica. En route, they drive at over 80 miles per hour. Going through a stop sign, they hit an old woman who is crossing the street without looking. They stop the car, pick up the woman's body, determine that she is dead, and then drive to a nearby lake where they dump the body and guns in the water.

Caruthers, Wilkins, and Jones are eventually found and charged for the killings of Prendergast and the old woman on the street. On cross-examination, Jones explains in tears that he had no idea his gun was loaded and that he did not know what the other two were up to before the gun went off. In their testimony, Wilkins and Caruthers explain that they loaded the gun as a joke and never intended to hurt — much less kill — anyone at all.

You are a juror. Suppose you believe Jones did not know his gun was loaded. Do you vote to convict him of murder for the death of Prendergast? Of involuntary manslaughter? Should he be punished at all for Prendergast's death?

Bearing in mind that an accomplice can be as guilty as (or more guilty than) the person who pulled the trigger, should the jury convict Caruthers and Wilkins of murdering Prendergast? Of involuntary manslaughter for Prendergast's death?

1. Involuntary Manslaughter By Criminal Negligence

There are many types of cases in which defendants have been found guilty of involuntary manslaughter because of criminal negligence. Most involve the use of cars or guns, but others have involved defendants who prescribed improper medical remedies for disease and/or injury. For example, in one case from the early part of this century, a man prescribed "hog's hoof brew, headache powder, and prayer" as a cure for pneumonia. The cure failed.

Speaking of prayer as a cure, many involuntary manslaughter cases involve situations where the defendant allegedly omitted to do something for someone to whom he owed a duty of care. In such cases, the court has to determine, first, whether the defendant owed a duty to the person who died. Second, if there was a duty, would any affirmative action on the part of the defendant have saved the victim's life? In other words, did the omission *cause* the death? Third, was the omission a breach of the duty? In other words, was the defendant criminally negligent or reckless?

But what if the person does not act because he believes in the power of prayer to heal? A person who fails to call a doctor under circumstances that constitute criminal negligence *can* be convicted of involuntary manslaughter without violating his or her First Amendment right to the free exercise of religion. Freedom of religion does not include the right to kill people. But, if a person believes that prayer is a more effective healer than earthly medicine, that might mean that the person was *not aware of the risk* he was subjecting the other person to — and therefore, that he was not reckless, as the Model Penal Code defines recklessness. If an objective standard (negligence) is required, the question becomes whether the defendant's conduct should be measured against that of the reasonable man, or the reasonable person of his/her religious convictions. Courts differ on questions like this.

Now consider the following hypothetical:

When his 10-year-old daughter Samantha falls ill with dyptheria, Mr. Josiah Plumestone, a devout Christian Scientist, refuses to call a doctor, telling friends that he will heal his daughter in an organized prayer session which he invites the whole town to attend. "Doctors will only make her worse," Plumestone says. Plumestone then goes away for two days to meditate and prepare himself for the prayer session. When he returns home, his daughter is dead. Plumestone is charged with and tried for manslaughter. The trial judge charges the jury as follows: "If you believe that the defendant honestly thought a doctor would make his daughter worse or not help her and that prayer would, this may excuse his failure to call a doctor. But, if you are satisfied that he also omitted to pray, and that the failure to pray caused the death, you may convict him." The jury convicts him. He appeals. What result should the appeals court reach?

Some courts say that ordinary tort negligence is sufficient for involuntary manslaughter, especially where a car or dangerous weapon is involved. Most courts hold that, in other situations, more than mere civil (tort) negligence must be proved for such a criminal conviction. Some courts hold that the defendant did *not* have to be aware of the risk in order to be convicted of involuntary manslaughter. Other courts take the view that it is unfair to punish a person with as serious a crime as involuntary manslaughter unless he was subjectively aware of the risk.

Should people be sent to prison, or otherwise subjected to the penalties of the criminal law, because they took a risk which a reasonable person would have recognized but which they, in fact, did not recognize? In an article titled "Negligent Behavior Should Be Excluded From Criminal Liability," Jerome Hall contends that "*punishing* a human being is a very serious matter. No one should be punished unless he has clearly acted immorally." But why does Hall assume that a person who *negligently* causes the death of another has not acted "immorally"? Hall answers by saying that, "although many persons are frequently blamed, this does not warrant a leap from that commonplace fact to the conclusion that punishment for negligence is justified. Important differences exist between . . . . raising an eyebrow and putting a man in jail."[1]

What is the position of the Model Penal Code on this issue? The drafters of the code considered the problem at length, noting the argument of many lawyers that "inadvertent negligence is not a sufficient basis for criminal conviction, both on the utilitarian ground that threatened sanctions cannot influence the inadvertent actor and on the moral ground that criminal punishment should be reserved for cases involving moral fault."[2] Ultimately, the code drafters recommended a separate homicide category — negligent homicide — for killings when the defendant was not aware of the risk of which a reasonable person would have been aware. No one can be convicted of murder *or* manslaughter under the Model Penal Code unless they were *subjectively* at fault (in other words, unless they were *at least reckless*), but they can be convicted of criminally negligent homicide for such inadvertent risk creation under the code.

Where negligence *does* suffice for a criminal conviction of manslaughter or some such crime, how is negligence *proved*?

Consider the following case:

State vs. Hernandez
Missouri Court of Appeals, 1991, 815 S.W.2d 67

A jury found Pedro Hernandez (defendant) guilty of involuntary manslaughter.

[On September 12, 1988, Cecil Barrymore was killed when the truck in which he was riding as a passenger collided with a van driven by the defendant. When asked at the scene whether he had been drinking, defendant said he had drunk "a 12-pack and some whiskey."]

There were stickers and pins attached to the visor [of the defendant's van which had] . . . various slogans . . . on them:

"The more I drink, the better you look";

"Reality is for those who can't stay drunk";

"A woman drove me to drink. I can't thank her enough";

Defendant contends that the trial court erred in admitting into evidence the . . . "drinking slogans." He argues that [they] ". . . were used to try to show him to be the 'type' of person who would commit the crime in question."

In order for evidence to be relevant, it must logically tend to support or establish a fact or issue between the parties. The elements of the offense of involuntary manslaughter that were required to be proven were . . . that defendant acted with criminal negligence and . . . that, in so doing, defendant caused Cecil Barrymore's death. [Under the relevant state statute,] a person acts with criminal negligence when he fails to be aware of a substantial and unjustifiable risk [of which a reasonable person would have been aware.]

The state argues that the drinking slogans are relevant because the remarks show that the defendant *"knew* that drinking large amounts of alcohol could distort . . . his driving skills."

That argument fails because the defendant's knowledge of the effect of alcohol on him was not an issue . . . . The state did not have to prove that the defendant knew of the effects of alcohol on him.

The state also argues that the drinking slogans were relevant because "they . . . indicated that he approved of excessive drinking." That is another way of saying that . . . he is a bad person . . . . Reputation or character testimony is admissible only when a defendant has put his own reputation in issue.

The trial court erred in admitting evidence of the drinking slogans . . . . The conviction . . . is reversed.

2. Reckless Murder

Under some circumstances, if a person takes a *big* risk, which results in the death of another person, the crime is murder. Murder convictions have been sustained in cases in which the defendant fired a gun into a room which he knew was occupied by more than one person, shot at moving cars or trains, drove at very high speeds on busy streets, and shook an infant so hard that it suffocated. In none of these cases did the defendant *intend* (in model-penal-code terms, have knowledge or purpose) the death. Yet, the law sometimes says that unjustified extreme risk taking, which happens to result in death, is murder.

When an *intentional act* (like shooting or speeding in a car) causes an *unintended death*, when is the crime involuntary manslaughter and when is it murder? The answer seems to depend, among other things, on the degree of risk. Thus, for instance, if I drive at 70 miles an hour in a 55 mile an hour zone, and hit another car, killing someone, I probably would be guilty of involuntary manslaughter at most. But if I were to drive at 80 miles an hour on the wrong side of the highway in a 55-mile per hour zone, and thereby hit and kill someone, that could well be murder.

It would be nice if we could *quantify* the degree of risk for each crime. For instance, we could say that a 1-to-5% chance of death is involuntary manslaughter, but if the chance is more than 5%, it is murder. But courts consistently refuse to accept such quantitative limitations. Justice Holmes summed up the dilemma with his usual acuity in a 1906 case:

> I have heard it suggested that the difference is one of degree. I am the last man in the world to quarrel with a distinction simply because it is one of degree. Most distinctions, in my opinion, are of that sort, and are none the worse for it.[3]

As in involuntary manslaughter, the question is often debated whether the defendant must consciously be aware of the risk to be convicted of murder. The Model Penal Code says yes. So too did Sir James Fitzjames Stephen in his famous 19th-century *History of the Criminal Law of England*. But Holmes, as we have seen from the case of the kerosene-soaked woman, was the most articulate advocate of using an objective standard to convict of murder. In Holmes' view, for instance, if a person were to go to the roof of a building and throw a heavy beam off the roof in broad daylight, thereby killing someone, this should be murder, regardless of whether the defendant knew of the risk his action posed, if a reasonable person would have been aware of the risk.

This issue only really comes up when defendants are less intelligent or more forgetful than the reasonable man. A special difficulty arises when the defendant is not aware of the risk because he is drunk. The Model Penal Code recommends that such drunken unawareness is irrelevant (Sec. 2.08 (2)):

> When recklessness establishes an element of an offense, if the actor, due to self-induced intoxication, is unaware of a risk of which he would have been aware had he been sober, such unawareness is immaterial.

In other words, according to the Model Penal Code, if a person gets drunk and drives extremely recklessly, thereby killing someone, he can be guilty of murder, and he will not be able to defend by saying he was not aware of the risk, as long as he would have been aware of the risk if sober.

Note that the Model Penal Code requires more than subjective awareness of the risk (in cases other than intoxication) for murder. It requires recklessness plus "extreme indifference to the value of human life." Many states follow the code's lead in requiring what is sometimes called "an abandoned and malignant heart" for a murder conviction based on recklessness.

So much for unintentional killings based on risk taking —

involuntary manslaughter through criminal negligence (and/or recklessness), and murder through criminal recklessness (and/or negligence). Under what circumstances can a person be guilty of manslaughter or murder when he was *not* at fault at all?

The next chapter addresses this issue.

NOTES

1. Jerome Hall, "Negligent Behavior Should Be Excluded From Criminal Liability," 63 *Colum. L.Rev.* 632 (1963)

2. American Law Institute, Model Penal Code and Commentaries, Comment to Sec. 210.4 at 86 (1980).

3. *Haddock v. Haddock*, 201 U.S. 562 (1906), Holmes dissenting.

CHAPTER EIGHT

Misdemeanor Manslaughter and Felony Murder

Re-read the hypothetical about Caruthers, Wilkins, and Jones on pages 81 and 82 at the start of the previous chapter. Suppose that speeding is a misdemeanor and that armed robbery is a felony. Should the defendants be guilty of manslaughter for the death of the old woman on the road? Of murder for her death? Under what circumstances does a killing, however accidental, become criminal homicide if caused by or in the course of another crime?

1. The Misdemeanor-Manslaughter Rule

About 1260 AD, the famous English jurist and scholar Bracton wrote that an unintended killing in the course of any unlawful act is criminal homicide.[1] Much later, as we have seen, the law came to divide criminal homicide into murder and manslaughter, and, later still, manslaughter came to be divided into voluntary manslaughter and involuntary manslaughter. In time, it came to be recognized that negligence or recklessness was only one of the ways in which a killing could be involuntary manslaughter. A killing, however accidental, in the course of an unlawful act would also constitute involuntary manslaughter. Thus was born what is sometimes called "**unlawful act manslaughter**."

The term "unlawful act" is a vague one. Some statutes specifically limit it to "crimes not amounting to a felony." Misdemeanors are certainly included in the term. In fact, sometimes the rule of unlawful act involuntary manslaughter is referred to as the **misdemeanor-manslaughter rule** — a counterpart of the felony-murder rule. If you are committing a misdemeanor and a death results, it is automatically manslaughter. For example, if you are speeding and you hit and kill a pedestrian, because of your speeding, this might well be involuntary manslaughter automatically. If you punch someone (criminal battery, a misdemeanor) and they fall down and, hitting their head, die, this might well be involuntary manslaughter automatically.

But can the phrase "unlawful act" also include acts that are morally wrong — offensive to society — but not strictly crimes at all? Some courts have said yes. In *Commonwealth v. Mink*, defendant, attempting to kill herself, accidentally killed her fiancé when he tried to stop her. The court said this was automatically manslaughter because attempted suicide, although not a crime, *is* an "unlawful act" for the purposes of this doc-trine.[2] Other courts have held that only misdemeanors which are *malum in se*, as opposed to *malum prohibitum*, can qualify as the "unlawful act" which triggers the misdemeanor-manslaughter rule. For instance, in one 19th-century case, a bartender who sold alcohol to a drunk man was held not guilty of unlawful act involuntary manslaughter when the drunken patron fell and killed himself, because the offense of selling liquor to intoxicated persons was only punishable by fine or loss of license (not prison) and was thus *malum prohibitum*.[3]

Suppose the underlying misdemeanor is strict liability. For instance, suppose that, in the case of the stuck cruise control device, the car had hit and killed someone. Should the driver, who was guilty of the strict liability offense of speeding, be automatically guilty of manslaughter too? Suppose that a druggist accidentally mislabels a drug and sells it to someone who takes it and dies. Should that be manslaughter even if the druggist was very careful — in other words, if he took every precaution that a reasonable druggist would have taken — on the grounds that, because he was guilty of the strict liability offense of selling impure drugs (misdemeanor), he is automatically guilty of manslaughter of the unlawful act variety?

Because of the apparent harshness of the unlawful act doctrine, courts have developed limitations on it. One of the most important of those limitations is *causation*. The mere fact that a death occurred while a defendant was committing a misdemeanor does not mean he is guilty of manslaughter. The misdemeanor must generally be said to *cause* the death. For instance, suppose you are driving a car without having renewed your license. Driving carefully, you nevertheless hit and kill a pedestrian. A court will probably say that this is *not* unlawful act manslaughter because the misdemeanor (driving after the expiration of the license) did not *cause* the death.

Actually, the issue of causation is more complicated than this, however. Suppose that in the Caruthers hypothetical, the defendants, after speeding at 80 mph, slowed down to a legal speed after sensing that they had eluded the police. And *then* they struck and killed the old lady in the road. In a sense, one can argue that the misdemeanor (speeding) *did* cause the death, in as much as the defendants would not have been in that place at that time and thus would not have hit the old lady if they had not been previously speeding. But is that enough to make the killing automatically manslaughter? A court might well say no, reasoning that the killing was remote in time and place from the misdemeanor (speeding) and thus not the **proximate cause** (even if it was the **but-for cause**) of the death.

Does it matter if the victim's death was not foreseeable? Does it matter if the defendant, although speeding, would not have been able to avoid hitting her even if he had been driving at a legal speed? On these issues, courts sometimes draw a line, again, between *malum prohibitum* and *malum in se* misdemeanors, or at least between misdemeanors that are not "inherently dangerous" and those that are. If the misdemeanor is *malum prohibitum*, courts often say that the defendant is only guilty if the victim's death was reasonably foreseeable. This does not require that the defendant foresaw the death, but only that a reasonable person would have foreseen it. It also does not require that it was reasonably foreseeable that this particular victim would die in this particular way, but only that the victim was a member of a general class of persons for whom death from the defendant's action was reasonably foreseeable. For instance, to return to the Caruthers hypothetical, if you are speeding down a busy street at 80 mph, it is reasonably foreseeable that you will hit and kill *someone*.

But, you say, the old lady was *contributorily negligent*, to use an expression from the law of torts, now often replaced by the concept of comparative negligence, because she stepped off the curb without looking. Is that fact relevant? It is well settled that contributory negligence is not a defense in criminal law. But the victim's carelessness may still be relevant if it shows that the defendants' action was not the legal *cause* of the death. Suppose it is clear that, even though the defendants were speeding when they struck her, they would not have been able to avoid hitting her if they had been driving within the speed limit? Did their speeding, then, cause the death?

If the speeding misdemeanor is treated as *malum prohibitum* (or, in the words of some state's laws, not inherently dangerous), the court will probably say that the speeding did *not* cause the death if they would have hit and killed the woman even if they had not been speeding. Put differently, the unlawful excess of their behavior (the extent to which they were exceeding the speed limit) was not the cause of her death.

But suppose the misdemeanor was not speeding but drunk driving? Many courts hold that drunk driving, unlike ordinary speeding, is *malum in se*, not *malum prohibitum*. Thus, they say, if you get drunk and drive and kill someone, it is automatically manslaughter even if you would not have been able to avoid the accident if you were sober! In other words, if you are committing a *malum in se* misdemeanor, like drunk driving, and you *unintentionally* kill someone, that is manslaughter regardless of whether the harm was foreseeable and regardless of whether the misdemeanor "caused" the victim's death.

What other misdemeanors are *malum in se*, for these purposes, besides drunk driving? Intentional battery is another example. If I punch you, intending only to knock you down, and you fall and hit your head on a nail and die, many courts will say that is involuntary manslaughter (of the unlawful act type) even if I did not and *could not* reasonably have foreseen your death from my act. If I am fighting with you and you cut yourself in the fight and from the cut you unexpectedly develop tetanus from which you die, many courts will say that this is automatically manslaughter. The same applies if you, unbeknownst to me, are a hemophiliac or have a thin skull and die from my cutting you or hitting you on the head.

What about a criminal assault? Suppose that, intending to

scare you but not kill or injure you, I point a knife at you and say, "You die tomorrow!" Terrified, you drop dead from a heart ailment that I had no reason to know you had. That could be involuntary manslaughter, if the state defines an assault as a *threatened battery*.

What is the future of the doctrine of unlawful act manslaughter (the misdemeanor-manslaughter rule)? The Model Penal Code recommends its abolition. So too do many legal scholars. As LaFave and Scott note in their treatise on Criminal Law, there is "no logical reason for inflicting manslaughter punishment on one who unintentionally kills another simply because he is committing a traffic violation, unless it makes sense to punish the one-in-a-thousand traffic violation, which by bad luck produces an unexpected death, far more severely than the nine hundred and ninety-nine violations which happily do not produce any such devastating result."[4]

Inspired by the Model Penal Code's example, many states have abolished this rule. Still, many still retain it, in one form or another. And a much more enduring rule permits punishment of *murder* when the defendant kills in the course of a felony. It is to the genesis, rationale, and limitations on this rule — the Felony-Murder Rule — that we now turn.

2. Felony Murder: Origins and Historical Development of the Rule

In the seventeenth century, the English jurist Coke, who became famous for quarreling with Kings and their defenders in an age of parliamentary feuds with the monarchy which ultimately led to Civil War and the beheading of the English king, wrote in his *Institutes of the Laws of England* that

> if A, meaning to steale a Deere in the Park of B, shooteth at the Deere, and by the glance of the arrow killeth a boy that is hidden in the bush, this is murder, for that the act was unlawful, although A had no intent to hurt the boy, nor knew not of him. But if B the owner of the Park had shot at his own Deere, and without any ill intent had killed the boy by the glance of his arrow, this had been homicide by misadventure, and no felony.[5]

According to the **felony-murder rule**, in its original and pure form, if you are committing a felony and, in the course of that felony, you cause another person's death, that is murder. The state does not have to prove any of the elements of murder. It does not matter if you were not negligent or not at fault. It does not matter how serious the felony was, or whether death or injury was remotely foreseeable. Murder thus becomes, in a sense, a strict liability offense. The *mens rea* for the felony substitutes for the *mens rea* for the murder and makes the killing automatically murder.

Why did the courts develop a rule like that? In those days, all felonies were punished by death. But if you only attempted to commit the felony and failed to complete it, you were only guilty of an attempted felony, and attempts — misdemeanors — were not felonies. If, however, your attempt resulted in the death of someone, the law called the crime murder and put you to death anyway. In other words, the felony murder rule originally emerged as a way of punishing attempted felonies resulting in death with the same penalty (the death penalty) reserved for successful felonies not resulting in death.[6]

The felony-murder rule might have seemed perfectly justifiable in an age in which there were few felonies and all of them got the death penalty. After all, why should the unsuccessful felon be treated more leniently than the successful one, especially if he kills someone in his unsuccessful attempt? But today, there are many, many more felonies. Few of them are punished by death. Many of them are not threatening to human life. Should the felony-murder rule apply today? Does it apply today?

England abolished the felony-murder rule by Act of Parliament in 1957. Other countries apparently never had it in the first place. But in America, the felony-murder rule, in various forms, survives in most states. America is thus probably the only country in the world where one can be guilty of murder for a purely accidental killing.

What are the arguments for the felony-murder rule? The first is that it helps deter accidental killings in the course of felonies. Justice Holmes once said that the rule might be justified if statistics showed that a disproportionate number of deaths resulted from the commission of felonies. But the statistics do not seem to suggest this. Recent studies, for instance, show that only one half of one percent of robberies end in homicide.[7] Moreover, how can one deter a pure accident?

The second rationale sometimes offered for the felony- murder rule is that it deters the *felony*. If a person is thinking of committing a felony, he will be less likely to commit it if he knows that, if his felony results in death, however careful he is, that will be murder. But is that a realistic assumption about would-be felons? In fact, does deterrence of any sort really explain, or justify, the rule? In his book *The Common Law*, Holmes concluded that it does not. Imagine, Holmes wrote, a man who, intending to steal some chickens (a felony), shoots at a chicken and accidentally hits a man, killing him. Does it make sense to say that, because he was committing a felony, his accidental killing automatically becomes murder?

> If the object of the rule is to prevent such accidents, it should make accidental killing with firearms murder, not accidental killing in the effort to steal; while if its object is to prevent stealing, it would do better to hang one thief in every thousand by lot.[8]

Other suggested rationales of the felony-murder rule include the argument that it reaffirms the sanctity of human life by expressing society's sense that, for example, "a robbery that causes death is more closely akin to murder than to robbery." Then too, it is sometimes said, it is too hard to prove an intentional killing, and too easy for a defendant to perjure himself into acquittal by saying, on the stand, that he killed by accident.

Ultimately, the felony-murder rule seems predicated on a sense of fairness: if you commit a felony, you should assume the risk that someone will be killed in the course of that felony. If someone is killed, you should pay the price — of murder.

But even its strongest advocates recognize that, under certain circumstances, applying the felony-murder rule in its strict form is unduly harsh. Suppose it is a felony to forge a check. While forging a check your pen slips and flies into the chest of a man sitting nearby, killing him. Should this be murder? Mindful of such potential inequities, courts and legislatures have developed limitations on the felony-murder doctrine.

3. Felony Murder Limitations: Inherently Dangerous Felonies

Many states now enumerate which felonies will give rise to a felony-murder conviction. Many others simply say that all felonies that are "inherently dangerous to life" can qualify. How do we determine whether a felony is inherently dangerous to life? Under one approach, we look at the felony in this particular case and ask whether it is inherently dangerous. Under another, we look at the felony in the abstract, divorced from the particulars of this case, and ask whether it is inherently dangerous — in other words, whether it is essentially impossible to commit this felony without posing a grave risk of death to human beings.

For instance, suppose that a person, committing the felony of practicing medicine without a license, tries to treat a person suffering from a serious heart condition with lemonade and music. The patient dies. Can the person who treated him be guilty of felony murder based on the felony of practicing without a license? If the court looks at the facts of the particular case to determine whether the felony is inherently dangerous, it is very likely that they will conclude that it is. But if they look at the felony in the abstract, the judges might well say that it is not. After all, it is possible to commit the felony of practicing medicine without a license without posing any threat to life at all — as, for instance, if one only treats hangnails or minor cuts and bruises.

Under this approach, the court might well refuse to allow the jury to be instructed about the felony-murder rule, and might require the state to prove the elements of murder in order to convict the defendant of that crime.

4. Felony Murder Limitations: Causation: "In the Commission of . . ."

Of course, it *does* matter, even under the strict felony-murder rule, whether your felony actually *causes* the death. Put differently, a mere coincidence of time and place has never been enough. For instance, suppose I break into your house with the intent to rob you (felony: burglary). Completely unaware of this break in, you suffer a heart attack upstairs in bed and die. No court, even following the strict common law rule, would say that this is felony murder. There must be some causal relationship between the felony and the death.

This is expressed in the part of the felony-murder rule which requires that the death have occurred "in the course of the felony." But what does "in the course of" really mean? Suppose the killing takes place at a time or place remote from the felony? Is it in the course of the felony?

Consider the following hypotheticals:

1) A would-be robber of a liquor store runs over and kills a pedestrian on his way to the store to rob it.

2) While robbing a bank, defendant accidentally shoots a bank teller. Six months later, after the defendant has escaped and is now living in another state, the teller dies from the wound.

3) Defendant is cleaning his gun when it goes off, accidentally killing his neighbor. Seeing his neighbor dead, defendant goes into his neighbor's house and robs him. Can he be guilty of felony murder based on the felony of larceny?

Most courts look at three things to determine whether a killing was "in the course of" the felony:

a. **time** — How remote in time was it? This is not always easy. For one thing, it is not always clear when the felony begins and ends. A robbery, for instance, technically begins when the defendant takes possession of and moves the property. Does that mean that if a robber is reaching for a bag of money in a bank and shoots and kills a bank guard at that moment, it isn't felony murder because the felony had not yet begun? Arson, for instance, technically begins when the building first catches fire. Does it continue as long as the fire burns? Would it be felony murder if a fireman is killed in trying to put out the blaze?

b.**place** — If the killing occurs at a place remote from the scene of the felony, that is a relevant factor, though not dispositive. In nearly all states, a killing in <u>flight</u> from a felony is still "in furtherance of the felony" and thus subject to the rule.

c. **causal connection** — Many courts require more than *but-for* causation. They also require some foreseeability. Others do not. Which approach is preferable?

In conclusion, in interpreting the "in the course of the felony" requirement for felony murder, most courts say that the felony begins when the defendant takes steps sufficient to constitute an attempt at the crime. We will see more on the law of attempt later, but for now it is enough to know that this generally means a substantial step toward execution of the crime. Thus, for example, if a bank robber's gun were to go off, accidentally killing someone just after the robber demanded the money but before any money was actually handed over, a court following the felony-murder rule could convict the robber of felony murder even though the crime of robbery was not yet complete — there had been no carrying away or "asportation" of the property (more on the elements of common law larceny and robbery later). On the other extreme, the felony is regarded as continuing while the defendant is in flight from the commission of the felony, at least until he or she reaches a place of relative safety. Thus a gun fight resulting in the death of a police officer or an innocent bystander several miles from the scene of the crime could be the basis of a felony-murder conviction if the killing occurs while the felon or felons are still trying to make their escape. In the end, the killing must occur within what is sometimes called the *res gestae* (Latin for things done or happened) of the crime — during attempt, during the felony itself, or during escape.

On the issue of foreseeablity, bear in mind that practically all courts require proximate causation as well as *but-for* causation, but some seem to define proximate causation to require foreseeability and some do not. For example, in many courts, an arsonist who sets fire to a person's house would be guilty of felony murder if an occupant of the house or a fireman or a visitor to the house is killed in the blaze, but the arsonist might not be guilty of felony murder if a looter were to break into the burning building and die or if one of the firemen were to die in a car crash on the way back to the firehouse.

Re-read the relevant portions of the Caruthers hypothetical and ask yourself again about whether the killing of the old lady on the road is "in the course of" the felony of armed robbery.

5. Felony Murder Limitations: The Merger Doctrine

Recall the *Thornton* case, about the second-year law student who shoots and kills his wife's lover after waiting outside the house for an hour with his camera. The court there said the crime was voluntary manslaughter. But if the felony-murder rule applies, wouldn't the crime be felony murder? After all, voluntary manslaughter is a felony. In the course of this felony, a man was killed. So, it is automatically murder. Right?

If this result seems odd, it is because such a result would totally abolish the crime of voluntary manslaughter. Voluntary manslaughter is always a felony. If, every time a person was guilty of only voluntary manslaughter we could use that felony as the underlying felony for a felony-murder conviction, the

mitigating plea of voluntary manslaughter — and thus an important part of the gradation of criminal homicides — would be gone.
All voluntary manslaughters would automatically escalate into
murders. Thus, courts have *uniformly* held that the felony of
voluntary manslaughter *merges* with the homicide, so that it
cannot be used as the underlying felony which will make the
homicide felony murder.

Beyond the question of manslaughter, courts have had a
more difficult time deciding which felonies merge with the
homicide, thus making it impossible to use them as the basis for
a felony-murder conviction. Suppose the felony is assault with a
deadly weapon. For instance, suppose a husband and wife are
quarreling and the husband pulls out a gun and shoots his wife,
killing her. He is guilty of the felony of assault with a deadly
weapon. Is he also automatically guilty of murder under a felony-
murder theory? In other words, should we allow the prosecution
to use the fact of the felony, admittedly an inherently dangerous
one, to make the killing automatically felony murder, so that the
prosecution does not have to prove *mens rea* or any of the
traditional elements of murder? On these facts, the California
Supreme Court said not in the 1969 case of *People v. Ireland*. The
felony of aggravated battery cannot be the basis for a felony-
murder conviction, the court said; in other words, it does merge
with the homicide.

If assault with a deadly weapon merges with homicide, what
about burglary? Recall that burglary is defined under the common law as breaking and entering a dwelling at night *with intent
to commit a felony* inside the dwelling. Contrary to popular mis-
conception, the intended felony inside the dwelling does not have
to be larceny or robbery. It could be assault with intent to kill.
What if a person breaks into my house tonight with an intent to
kill me (felony of burglary) and then does kill me? Can that be
automatically felony murder, so that the prosecution is relieved
of the necessity of proving *mens rea* and the elements of murder?
Or does the felony of burglary, in such a case, *merge* with the
homicide?

On facts like these, the California Supreme Court found
merger (and thus no felony murder) in *People v. Wilson*, also in
1969. In a subsequent case, *People v. Sears*, the court held that, even
if the burglar broke in with the intent to assault and kill one
person and then, once inside, killed someone else, still the felony

of the burglary merged with the homicide and could not serve as the underlying felony for a felony-murder charge.

It is important to understand that *Wilson* and *Sears*, and cases reaching the same result in other states, do *not* say that burglary can never be the underlying felony which makes a killing felony murder. They are only speaking of the situation in which the breaking-in is burglary only because of an intent to commit an assault or a homicide inside the dwelling. They have no obvious application to other cases of burglary — where the intent is to steal or to rape, for instance, inside the home.

On the other hand, the rationale of this whole line of cases — in California, and other states — appeared to be that any felony which included within it an assault with a deadly weapon would merge with the homicide and could not be used as the underlying felony for a felony-murder conviction. This would include robbery. After all, robbery is nothing more than larceny with force or threat of force. It could also be interpreted to include rape, and all other violent felonies.

The California Supreme Court rejected these possible expansions of the merger doctrine in *People v. Burton* (1971). There, the court held that the merger doctrine did not apply if the felony involved an assault with an "independent felonious purpose" — independent of the homicide. Thus, for example, a rape involves an assault. But the purpose of the assault — non-consensual sexual intercourse — is distinct from homicide (killing). Thus if a rapist kills his victim during the rape, the rape *can* be the underlying felony that makes the killing felony murder. The same logic applies to robbery, or burglary where robbery is the intended crime inside the dwelling. These crimes include an intended assault, but the purpose of the assault — to obtain possession of and carry away the personal property of another — is totally distinct from homicide. Thus, these felonies *do not merge.* So said the California court.

Consider the following hypotheticals. Do they illustrate a paradox in the application of the merger doctrine to felony murder?

1) A enters B's home with intent to steal B's stereo. As he breaks in, A's gun accidentally goes off, killing B. A is guilty of felony murder for B's death. The state does *not* have to prove that A killed B with malice aforethought.

2) A enters B's home with intent to shoot B. A enters and

kills B (or C). A is *not* guilty of the felony murder of B or C, because the felonies of burglary and assault with a deadly weapon merge with the homicide. The state *does* have to prove that A killed B (or C) with malice aforethought in order to convict A of murdering B or C.

      3) A beats his small child with intent to discipline but not kill him. The beating kills the child. A is guilty of felony murder based on the underlying felony of child abuse (*People v. Jackson*). The state does *not* have to prove malice aforethought.

      4) A beats his small child with intent to kill. He does kill him. A is *not* guilty of felony murder based on the underlying felony of child abuse, because the felony merges with the homicide. (*People v. Smith*). The state *does* have to prove malice aforethought to convict A of murdering his child.

You should note that some states do not follow the merger rule the way California does. For instance, in New York and in a majority of other states, burglary does *not* merge with homicide — and thus <u>can</u> be the underlying felony for a felony-murder conviction — even if the only reason the breaking and entering is burglary is because of an intent to assault and kill someone inside the dwelling. Is this result preferable to that reached by the California court? The New York court explained its conclusion on the grounds that assaults inside a home are more dangerous than assaults outside. They involve more risk of harm to third parties, and the intended victim has less opportunity to escape. Thus, it makes sense to say that an assault *outdoors* cannot support a felony-murder charge when it results in killing, while a burglary based on intent to commit that same assault *indoors* can.

Many commentators, however, find this argument illogical. Are outdoors assaults (which merge with the homicide) not dangerous? Even an assault with an intent to kill, outdoors, will merge with the homicide and defeat a felony-murder claim! What could be more "dangerous" than that? Moreover, is the purpose of the merger doctrine to identify the least dangerous felonies and make the felony-murder rule applicable to them, while making it inapplicable to more dangerous felonies? Not really. The purpose of the merger rule is to preserve the integrity of the homicide grading system. If we allowed assault with a deadly weapon to be the underlying felony that makes a killing felony murder, then all homicides that result from assaults with a deadly weapon would automatically be felony murder. But nearly all homicides result from assaults with a deadly weapon! So, nearly all homicides would be felony murder! We wouldn't bother with voluntary manslaughter pleas, or questions of lack of intent or recklessness, or accident. In all these cases the defendant would be guilty of murder by a felony-murder theory. It is to avoid *this* sort of result that the merger doctrine was created — merging into the homicide those felonies that depend *solely* on an assault or on killing itself to be felonious. But, under this reasoning, it should not matter whether the intended assault takes place inside or outside the home. Thus, many have reasoned, if an assault outside the home would merge, so too should burglary based on an intended assault inside the home. Neither should permit a charge of felony murder.

As I have said, a majority of states take this view, but it is by no means an uncontroversial position. In the end, it has been said that the application of the merger rule and the rule requiring that the felony be inherently dangerous has the anomalous result that, in many ways, only felonies of moderate seriousness can serve as the basis for the felony-murder rule. The *least* dangerous felonies (forgery, embezzlement, and so on) will be excluded because of the inherently dangerous felony requirement. At least some of the *most* dangerous felonies (assault with intent to kill, for instance) will be excluded because of the merger doctrine. Many lawyers question whether it makes sense to limit felony murder to felonies in the middle.

What felonies are left? Many felony murder statutes specifically enumerate which felonies can serve as the basis for a felony-murder charge. As a general rule, however, law students are often taught that a list of the common law felonies that can usually give rise to the felony murder doctrine can be remembered by memorizing the acronym MRS. BAKER — Mayhem, Rape, Sodomy, Burglary, Arson, Kidnapping, Escape (from official custody), and Robbery.

6. Felony Murder Limitations: Liability of Co-Felons

Suppose that two people, Nathan Garideb and Phil Jenkins, are robbing a bank. Garideb shoots and kills a bank guard. Assuming that there is a felony, Garideb will be guilty of felony murder, even if he had no intent to kill the guard and even if the killing was purely accidental. But what about Jenkins? Can he be convicted of felony murder for the death of the bank guard too?

Courts uniformly say yes, for two reasons. One is that Garideb was acting as Jenkins' *agent*, and so Jenkins is responsible for Garideb's acts. The other is that Jenkins' actions in participating in the bank robbery set in motion the chain of events which *proximately caused* the death of the bank guard, and so Jenkins is equally responsible for the killing.

Suppose, however, that Garideb had not told Jenkins that he was carrying a gun and that the shooting was completely unexpected. In some cases, courts will reject the applicability of the felony-murder rule to co-felons where the killing was completely beyond the common purpose.

Now suppose the facts in the hypothetical are different. On their way out of the bank after the robbery, Jenkins and Garideb are spotted by a police officer, who shoots at them, missing and killing an innocent bystander. Can the felons be convicted of felony murder for this killing?

Virtually all courts agree that if the felons had pulled the innocent person in front of them as a **human shield** and the police officer had shot at them, killing the innocent person, the felons *would* be guilty of felony murder. The action of the felons in making the person a shield is enough to make them both guilty of felony murder for the death. But what if it is not a shield situation? What if the officer's bullet simply missed the felons and hit the innocent person by mistake?

In circumstances like these, courts differ, depending on whether they adopt the agency theory or the proximate cause theory of felony murder. Under the **agency theory**, followed by a majority of states, a felon is only guilty of killings committed by one of his agents. His co-felon is his agent, of course. But a police officer is not. Neither would a third party be. Thus, if a bank teller pulled out a gun and, shooting at the robbers, hit and killed someone, that would not be felony murder under the agency theory because the bank teller is not an agent of the felons.

Under the **proximate cause theory**, by contrast, what matters is not who did the shooting. Rather, what counts is whether the shooting was a forseeable consequence, a proximately caused consequence, a direct consequence, of the felony. Would the killing have occurred if the felony had not occurred? Was the killing a natural and probable consequence of the felony?

Now let's change the hypothetical again. Suppose that, instead of missing and hitting an innocent person, the police officer or bank teller successfully shot and killed one of the felons. Could the other felon be guilty of felony murder of his co-felon? If the court follows the agency theory, obviously there cannot be felony murder because, again, the teller or officer is not an agent of the felons. But what if the court follows proximate cause?

Even courts following the proximate cause approach have often been reluctant to find the other felon guilty of felony murder in a situation like this. In Pennsylvania, for example, the same court that had decided that, when a policeman fired at a felon and killed another policeman, there *could* be felony murder on a theory of proximate cause (*Commonwealth v. Almeida*)[9] held there could *not* be felony murder if the policeman shot one of the robbers to death instead. In the famous case of *Commonwealth v. Redline*, the court held that murder *cannot* be based on justifiable homicide: since the shooting by the police officer of the felon was justifiable homicide, the surviving felon could not be guilty of felony murder:

> How can anyone . . . have a criminal charge lodged against him for the consequences of the lawful conduct of another person? The mere statement of the question carries with it its own answer.[10]

But there are difficulties with this reasoning. Is it always true that one cannot be guilty of murder for a lawful homicide of another person? The officer who slips the noose around the neck of the man condemned to be hanged is surely not guilty of criminal homicide when the man dies. But if someone perjures the condemned man to the gallows, that person can be guilty of murder. Moreover, wasn't the killing of the other officer in *Almeida* also a lawful homicide? And yet, the same Pennsylvania court held that this was felony murder by the surviving felon. The court in *Redline* refused to overrule *Almeida*, making a distinction between justifiable homicide (officer kills felon: no felony murder by other felon) and excusable homicide (officer kills other officer: felony murder by other felon). But this distinction doesn't seem to explain the difference satisfactorily.

In the end, the rationale of the *Redline* rule, now followed by most courts, though not all — the rule that "there is **no felony murder liability when one of the *felons* is shot and killed by the victim, a police officer, or a bystander**"[11] — seems predicated on the theory that it is not *fair* to convict one felon for the unintended death of his co-felon, who was, after all, a willing participant in the felony in the first place. Judge Posner has criticized this theory, saying that the "lives of criminals are not completely worthless."

Courts that use the agency approach to felony murder sometimes do permit one felon to be guilty of murder of his co-felon when the co-felon is shot by a police officer or victim by using what is sometimes called the theory of **vicarious liability murder**. This approach is illustrated by the case of *Taylor v. Superior Court*, in which the Supreme Court of California ruled that an accomplice waiting outside in a getaway car was guilty of *first degree* murder for the death of his co-felon at the hands of the victim of the robbery, who opened fire when the felons entered her store and threatened to kill her husband. The court there speaks of "vicarious liability murder." But this doctrine is perhaps more properly understood as a species of *reckless* murder. It was because the defendants in *Taylor* were reckless — by pointing the gun at the store owners and "chattering insanely" about an "execution," although they did not start the shooting — that the court held them guilty of the murder of their co-felon. But note that reckless murder is usually *second-degree* murder. In *Taylor*, the court found *first-degree* murder, explaining very obscurely in a footnote that, in such a situation, the felony-murder statute is triggered, thus determining the degree of the homicide. But the court had already noted that the defendant could not be guilty of felony murder because the agency theory was used. So why does the court use the felony-murder statute (which made killings in "furtherance of a felony" *first-degree murder*) to determine the degree (first-degree) of the crime?

7. Conclusions: Felony Murder

Some of the problems posed by the felony-murder rule seem magnified by the fact that courts are often not enthusiastic about the rule in the first place. Other difficulties and complexities, however, seem inherent in the rule itself, and would, it appears, have to be addressed by any court following the rule, however enthusiastically. In the last analysis, the issue is whether it is possible for the finely tuned, grading structure of the law of criminal homicide to coexist with a strict liability rule that makes the degree of the crime depend, not on *mens rea* for the killing, but on the related occurrence of another crime.

In introducing the subject of two or more felons, our discussion of the felony-murder rule leads us to the next issue: when should one be guilty of crimes committed by another person?

In general the theory of vicarious liability, so essential to the law of torts, is foreign to the criminal law. Guilt is personal to the accused. You are responsible for what *you* have done. But there are very important exceptions to this rule. One is the doctrine of complicity, otherwise known as the law of aiding and abetting. The other grows out of the law of conspiracy, a partnership in crime. It is to these two topics, and the general subject of group crimes, that we now turn.

NOTES

1. Bracton, *De Legibus et Consuetudinibus Angliae*, c. 1260.

2. *Commonwealth v. Mink*, 123 Mass. 422 (1877).

3. *State v. Reitze*, 86 N.J.L. 407 (1914), cited in LaFave and Scott, *Criminal Law*, p. 677.

4. LaFave and Scott, p. 683.

5. Quoted in Dressler, *Cases and Materials on Criminal Law*, (St. Paul: West, 1994), p. 257.

6. *Ibid.* p. 258, note 74.

7. See *Enmund v. Florida*, 485 U.S. 782 (1982)

8. Quoted in LaFave, p. 640.

9. *Commonwealth v. Almeida*, 362 Pa. 596, 68 A.2d 595 (1949), cited in LaFave and Scott, *Criminal Law*, p. 628, n. 45. Actually, the facts of *Almeida* suggested that both the police officer and the felons were shooting, and that it was not entirely clear whether the fatal shot killing one officer was fired by the other officer by mistake or by the felons. The court thus reasoned that the felony-murder liability of the other felon should not depend on the accident of who actually fired the fatal shot.

10. *Commonwealth v. Redline*, 391 Pa. 486, 137 A.2d 472 (1958).

11. See LaFave and Scott, p. 629.

CHAPTER NINE

Complicity: Aiding and Abetting

The hypothetical about the students' holdup at the school at the start of Chapter Seven reminds us that there may be more than one party to a crime. Under the common law, there were four categories of parties to a felony: the principal in the first degree, principal in the second degree, accessory before the fact, and accessory after the fact. Today, practically all states have abolished these distinctions, providing instead that all except accessories after the fact are treated as principals.[1]

What, then, do we mean by the term **accomplice**? An accomplice is generally considered to be any person who is responsible for the crimes of another, whether or not he was present at the scene of the crime. For instance, if I persuade you to kill someone and you do kill that person, I am an accomplice to murder. If you rob a bank and I drive the get-away car, I am an accomplice to robbery. I am an accomplice in these cases because I **aided** and **abetted** the crime.

Aiding and abetting — otherwise called accomplice liability — is *derivative*. That is to say, the accomplice is *not* guilty of an independent offense called aiding and abetting. Rather, the accomplice is guilty of the *same crime* as the person who fired the shot or actually took the money. That is what it means to say that the law treats the accomplice as a principal. In the eyes of the law, the accomplice (one who aids and abets) has committed the same crime. The other person's act is his act. He is criminally responsible for the act of the other party whom he aided.

Does this mean that the accomplice is punished the same as the primary party? He can be, and often is. But courts usually have discretion to impose a less severe punishment on the aider and abettor than on the primary party. In some circumstances, courts will impose a *more* severe punishment on the accomplice, or even find him or her guilty of a more serious crime. For instance, suppose that Iago persuades Othello to kill his wife by falsely telling him she has been unfaithful to him. Othello, killing her in a furious rage, might be guilty only of voluntary manslaughter, or, at most, second-degree murder. But Iago, who coolly and with premeditation incited the killing, would probably be guilty of first-degree murder.

1. Actus Reus: Aiding and Abetting

What does one have to do to aid and abet a crime? Words of encouragement or even gestures can be enough, even if they take place long before the crime occurs. But if you merely intend to render aid and do not do anything, that is not sufficient. Neither is it sufficient for you to be at the scene of the crime, unless, by your mere presence you encouraged the commission of the crime — for example, by leading the other party to believe that, with superior numbers on his side, he could beat-up someone else or commit some other crime.

If you *do* provide assistance to the other party, it is not necessary that the other party know of the assistance. For instance, if A finds out that B intends to kill C on Main Street at noon on the 24th and, without telling B, A induces C to go to Main Street at that time so he will be killed by B, A may be guilty of aiding and abetting the murder of C (and thus be guilty of murder of C) if C goes and B does kill him.

Can one aid and abet by **omission**? Yes, if one has a duty to act. If a mother does not rescue her child when he is being beaten to death by a stranger or by her husband, she may be guilty of murder or manslaughter. If the owner of a car permits a drunken friend to drive his car at a dangerous speed, the owner may be guilty of reckless driving.

What if the husband would have beaten the child to death even if the mother had tried to intervene, or the drunken friend would have continued driving dangerously even if the car owner had tried to stop him? Normally in omissions cases, the omission must be the cause of the harm. But causation is *not* required in aiding and abetting, either for omissions or commissions. If the court finds that the mother's culpable omission assisted the killing of the child, or the car owner's culpable omission assisted the dangerous driving, the aider and abettor is guilty regardless of whether it can be shown that his omission caused the harm or not. Put differently, an aider and abettor is criminally responsible for the crimes of the primary party regardless of how small or trivial his assistance is. If you assist or encourage me in killing someone, in however small a way, and I do kill that person, you are also guilty of murder, provided you have the right *mens rea.* What is the "right *mens rea*"?

2. Mens Rea: Aiding and Abetting

It is not enough that one person assists or encourages another in the commission of a crime. To be guilty as an accomplice, that person must **intentionally** render the assistance or encouragement. He must, in other words, give the aid with the intent of encouraging or assisting the crime.

What does "intent" mean here? Some courts have said that knowledge is enough, and, in the early days, most said so. In a famous case in the 1930s, *United States v. Peoni,* Judge Learned Hand, who is probably the most distinguished judge in American history who never sat on the Supreme Court, said that purpose, not just knowledge, is required. The accomplice, Hand wrote, must "associate himself with the venture" as something he "wishes to bring about." Following this lead, the Model Penal Code, and most states today, require a purpose to aid and abet. Otherwise, courts sometimes adopt a compromise, holding purpose necessary when the crime is minor and/or the assistance is insignificant, but holding knowledge sufficient if the crime is serious and/or the assistance substantial. Thus, one who knowingly sells a dress to a prostitute will not be guilty of aiding and abetting prostitution unless he sells it with the conscious objective of encouraging the prostitution. But one who knowingly sells a gun to someone who intends to use it to kill someone could be guilty of murder by aiding and abetting, even if it could not be proved that the killing was his objective in making the sale.

Sometimes, even if a person has the requisite intent (whether defined as purpose, as in the Model Penal Code, or knowledge) to render the aid, and does render the aid, he is still not guilty of the crime because he does not have the *mens rea* for the crime. In other words, the aider and abettor must have *two* mental states: first, he must intend to render the assistance in the commission of the crime, and second, he must have the minimum *mens rea* required for the crime itself. For instance, suppose an undercover agent assists another person in the crimes of larceny and burglary by boosting him through a window into a home. He did assist the crime, and he did intend to assist it. But he did not intend to deprive the owner of his property. He did not have the *mens rea* for the crime. Thus he would not be guilty of burglary or larceny by aiding and abetting. This rationale has been applied to situations other than those involving undercover agents.

3. Aiding and Abetting Recklessness or Negligence

Suppose that A intentionally encourages B to drive A's car unsafely. B hits and kills someone. If B is guilty of reckless murder or involuntary manslaughter (of the reckless/negligent type), can A also be guilty of that crime, on a theory that he aided and abetted? At first blush, it would seem that he could not be, since aiding and abetting requires intent or purpose and reckless murder and involuntary manslaughter are, by definition, unintended. How can one intentionally encourage an unintentional act? But, as most courts have concluded, this reasoning is wrong. One can be guilty of aiding and abetting such crimes. If one intentionally encouraged the act that led to the unintended consequence, that is enough. As long as you had the *mens rea* for the substantive crime, that is enough. If your act of encouraging the person to drive unsafely was reckless, and if recklessness is sufficient for conviction of the offense, then you can be guilty of committing the offense by aiding and abetting.

Actually, in this hypothetical of A letting B drive his car

unsafely, many courts might find A guilty of the substantive offense without using a theory of aiding and abetting. If A turns over his car to B, knowing that B is an unsafe driver or is intoxicated, and B, driving the car, hits and kills someone, A may be guilty of involuntary manslaughter, not just as an aider and abettor, but as one who directly engaged in conduct that constituted the offense: A negligently (or recklessly) gave his car to someone, and that act caused the death.

The point is that causation *is* required if we are not using the aiding and abetting theory and not if we are. For example, the state, using an aiding and abetting theory, would not have to prove that A's encouragement of B to drive drunk was the cause of B's drunken driving or the cause of the accident. It would not be necessary for the state to show that the crime would not have happened but for the encouragement. But, if the state is not relying on aiding and abetting, and wants simply to say that A is directly guilty of involuntary manslaughter for his negligent act, it has to show that A's act caused the accident.

4. The Innocent Agency Doctrine

It is a well settled rule in the law of accomplice liability that there can be no guilty aider and abettor unless there is a guilty principal. More precisely, you cannot be guilty of aiding and abetting if no crime is actually committed.

Actually, this rule is more complicated. The aider and abettor *can* be tried and convicted even if the principal cannot be found, or cannot be brought to justice because he is dead. But what if the principal is actually tried and *acquitted* of the crime? Does that mean that "no crime" was actually committed, so that the alleged accomplice cannot be tried?

It depends on why the principal was acquitted. Let's say that A deliberately incites B, a mentally ill person, to kill C. When B does kill C, both B and A are tried for murder — B as principal and A as aider and abettor. If B is acquitted by reason of insanity, can A be tried and convicted? The answer is yes, if the court follows the innocent agency doctrine.

This doctrine is actually much older than contemporary complicity law. Under the old common law categories of complicity, a person could be guilty as the principal in the first degree even if he did not commit the offense with his own hands. If A opened a window in a house and used a stick to remove an item of personal property from inside the house, he could be guilty of burglary and larceny even though his own body never entered the house. If A trained his vicious dog to bite people and the dog did bite someone, killing that person, A could be guilty of criminal homicide. If A incited an insane person or a child to kill someone and the killing did take place, A could be guilty of murder.

In all these cases, the law said — and still says — that the person is guilty of committing the crime through another innocent instrumentality. Today, this innocent agency rule permits a person to be guilty of committing a crime through another innocent person.

But what if the crime is such that it could not be committed by the defendant, even if he acted alone. For instance, under the common law, a woman's husband cannot be guilty of raping her. What if her husband incites another man to rape his wife by falsely telling him that his wife was consenting? If the man who does the act is not guilty because, somehow, he really believed the woman was consenting, can the husband be guilty of rape by aiding and abetting? Or suppose a woman encourages a man to rape another woman. Can the woman be guilty of rape by aiding and abetting?

Suppose I deliberately encourage a married man to marry again by falsely telling him his marriage has been annulled. Am I guilty of bigamy by aiding and abetting?

Many states, and the federal complicity statute, say that there *can* be criminal liability in such situations of "non proxy-able offenses." Even though the statute requires that the crime be committed by certain persons or classes of persons, another person can commit the offense by aiding and abetting, or through the innocent agency doctrine, as long as the act would be a crime if performed directly by them or by some other person.

5. Conclusion: Aiding and Abetting

Aiding and abetting is one important way in which one person may be criminally responsible for acts done by another person. But what if two people *agree* to commit a crime. That agreement in itself is a crime. And if one of the parties then commits a *different crime* in furtherance of that criminal agreement, both of them may be guilty of that crime as well. For an analysis of that topic, we need to turn next to the law of conspiracy.

CHAPTER TEN

Conspiracy

A conspiracy is a partnership in crime. When two or more persons agree to commit a crime and begin to do something in execution of that agreement, they are already guilty of a crime — even if the "object crime" which they agreed to perform is never committed. For example, if you and I agree to kill someone, and you buy a gun for this purpose or call the intended victim to make sure he will be at home at the time we plan our attack, we are both guilty of conspiracy to murder, even if the killing never happens. If the killing does happen, we can both be guilty of both murder and conspiracy to murder.[1]

Conspiracy is a paradox. Why should we punish people just for the fact of collective action toward a crime? The usual reason given is that such group action makes the crime more likely to occur (because if one intended criminal backs out, there will always be another to perform) and more dangerous (other crimes may be committed in the course of the conspiracy).

States vary in the way they punish conspiracy. The *federal* conspiracy statute provides up to five years in prison for conspiracy, and also specifies that you cannot be sentenced to more prison time for conspiracy than you could have gotten for the object crime. For instance, if you conspire to commit petty theft, and the petty theft by itself would carry a maximum penalty of three years, you cannot get more than three years for the conspiracy to commit the petty theft. Not all states follow this lead. In some states, a conspiracy to commit a misdemeanor is a felony and punished more seriously than the misdemeanor. In some, conspiracy is punished the same as the object crime.[2] In most states, conspiracy is punished less than the object crime.

Conspiracy is a controversial area of criminal law, partly because of its somewhat sinister history. It was not one of the original common law crimes, but was created by Parliament in a very limited form during the reign of Edward I — called the English Justinian because, like the Roman Emperor Justinian of ancient times, he was a great lawgiver — around 1300 AD. But conspiracy really got started in England during the seventeenth century — a time of civil war and political chaos. The infamous Court of Star Chamber used conspiracy charges to convict many political opponents of the king. In our country's history, conspiracy laws have been used to convict members of labor unions and politically unpopular groups. Sometimes people are convicted of conspiring to do something which would not be a crime if done by one person. Under the antitrust laws for instance, a conspiracy in "restraint of trade" can consist of price cutting by two or more companies which would not be a crime if done by one company alone.

Conspiracy is also criticized because it can be so vague. As Justice Jackson put it in his famous concurring opinion in *Krulewitch v. United States*, conspiracy is an

> elastic, sprawling and pervasive offense . . . so vague that it almost defies definition [and] chameleon like [since it] takes on a special coloration from each of the many independent offenses on which it may be overlaid.[3]

Prosecutors love conspiracy. They love it because charging people with conspiracy gives them a number of important procedural and substantive law advantages.

1. Procedural Advantages of Conspiracy

a. Venue. The Sixth Amendment provides that the accused

has the right to trial in "the district wherein the crime shall have been committed." But in a conspiracy case, the crime is said to have been "committed" not only where the agreement was made or where the object crime was carried out, but also in any state or district where any one of the conspirators committed any act in furtherance of the conspiracy. Thus, as Justice Jackson observed in *Krulewitch*, the "government may, and often does, compel one to defend at a great distance from any place he ever did any act because some accused confederate did some trivial and by itself innocent act in the chosen district."

b. Hearsay Exception.

The hearsay rule generally means that an out-of-court statement is not admissible to prove the truth of the statement. But there are exceptions. One is the co-conspirator exception. An out-of-court statement by one conspirator, made during the course of the conspiracy, can be used against another co-conspirator. Statements by one conspirator are also admissible against other co-conspirators who join the conspiracy after the statement is made.

Usually the courts require independent evidence of the conspiracy first, before they will permit such a statement to be admissible for purposes of the co-conspirator exception to the hearsay rule. But sometimes courts will admit the statement without such evidence, instructing the jury that the admissibility of the statement is conditional on the prosecutor's presenting other evidence of conspiracy. This leads to the criticism, sometimes made, that the court is "bootstrapping" — proving conspiracy by evidence that is only admissible if there is a conspiracy.

c. Joint Trial.

When two or more people are charged with conspiracy, they can all be tried together in one trial. In such a setting, the probability of their all being convicted is greatly enhanced. Juries tend to believe that "birds of a feather flock together," and that if one of the defendants is guilty, they all must be.

d. Statute of Limitations.

The statute of limitations does not begin to run on conspiracy until the conspiracy is abandoned (more on abandonment later) or succeeds. And it is not necessarily "successful" as soon as the object crime is completed. If two people conspire to rob a series of banks and divide the loot among them, the conspiracy is not complete, and the statute of limitations does not begin to run, until all the banks are robbed and the loot is fully divided.

Moreover, the fact that a conspiracy lasts so long, in the eyes of the law, can have important additional advantages for the prosecution. The longer it lasts, the more likely it is that additional acts will be performed in additional locations, so that the venue choices for trial will be expanded. If more people join the conspiracy, more defendants can be added in one trial.

2. Substantive Law Advantages of Conspiracy

Conspiracy does two things. It makes it easier to punish incipient criminal activity than the law of attempt does.[4] And it makes it easier to punish group crimes than the law of aiding and abetting does.

a. Punishing Behavior Before It Reaches Attempt.

Under the common law, the only *actus reus* required for conspiracy is the agreement. The agreement is said to be the essence or "gist" of the crime of conspiracy. Moreover, the agreement does not have to be an "open covenant openly arrived at," as in Woodrow Wilson's League of Nations. It can be a tacit understanding. The court can infer the existence of an agreement from the behavior of the parties.

To say that the agreement can be inferred is not to say that an agreement need not be proved, however. If A and B happen to rob the same house on the same night, that does not make them guilty of conspiracy to rob unless they arranged their robbery beforehand.

This brings us to an important point about the difference between the law of conspiracy and the law of aiding and abetting. Is it possible for a person to aid and abet a crime without conspiring to do so? The answer is yes. Suppose I suggest to you that we murder someone. I show you how easy it would be and tell you how we can do it. You refuse to agree to such a scheme. Later, you use my ideas to kill the person yourself. We might not be guilty of conspiracy to murder because there was no agreement, but I could be guilty of aiding and abetting the murder because I encouraged it. As another example, suppose that, knowing that you intend to kill a particular person, and without telling you, I lure the victim to the scene, or make it more likely that he will be killed by drugging him so that he will not be able to resist the attack. I am guilty of aiding and abetting the murder, if it occurs, but I will not be guilty of conspiracy to murder because you and I never even discussed the crime. Similarly, if I am walking down the street and I see you killing someone and I spontaneously come to your aid, I will be guilty of aiding and abetting the murder if it succeeds, but probably not of conspiracy to murder unless there was a pre-existing arrangement between us that I would help.

If agreement is the essence of conspiracy, however, it is not always the only required part of the *actus reus*. In many states today, an overt act in execution of the agreement is also required. But the overt act does not have to come as close to the completed offense as an attempt would. It does not even have to be a crime. It can be an innocent act, like making a phone call or writing a letter. The overt act need only be performed by one of the conspirators. Moreover, it applies against people who join the conspiracy after the overt act was performed. For instance, let's say that a state requires both an agreement and an overt act for conspiracy. A and B agree to kill C. A then writes a letter to C, asking him to be at a particular place at a particular time so they can kill him. After this but before the killing, D, E, and F also agree to help out. Immediately on their agreement, D, E, and F are guilty of conspiracy (A and B were guilty as soon as A wrote the letter), because the overt act of A's letter writing is imputed to them as well.

The point of all this is that conspiracy can occur much earlier than an attempt. A telephone call to the victim would almost certainly not be enough for attempted murder, as we will see when we get to the law of attempt. But it would be enough for conspiracy. And, in some states, even the agreement itself, without anything more, is enough.[5]

b. **Punishing Group Crimes.**

Suppose that A and B agree to rob a grocery store. During the robbery, A unexpectedly pulls out a gun and shoots and kills the store owner. A and B are both guilty of robbery and conspiracy to rob. They are not guilty of conspiracy to murder because they never agreed on the killing. But are they both guilty of murder?

We have already seen one way that one person can be guilty

of a crime committed by another person: the doctrine of aiding and abetting (complicity). Using this doctrine, would B be guilty of murder in this hypothetical? Probably not, because, as we saw, aiding and abetting usually requires purpose (conscious objective), and it was presumably not B's purpose that A should kill. He did not even expect this act. But there is an alternative way in which a person can be guilty of a crime committed by another person. If one person conspires with another to commit a crime, he can be guilty not only of conspiracy but also of all reasonably foreseeable crimes committed by any of his co-conspirators in the course of the conspiracy.

The leading case that establishes this rule, followed in federal cases and in many states, is *Pinkerton v. United States*. In that case, Pinkerton was indicted for conspiring with his brother to evade taxes, but also for specific tax evasions committed by his brother while Pinkerton was in jail. Pinkerton argued that he could not be guilty of such crimes because he was in jail when they were committed. But the trial court ruled that he could be convicted of these crimes as long as they were in furtherance of the conspiracy of which he was a member. The Supreme Court of the United States affirmed, indicating in dictum that the result might be different if the crimes were not reasonably foreseeable. From this case, we get the Pinkerton Rule, followed in some states, i.e.: a conspirator is guilty of any substantive crimes committed by any of his fellow conspirators, if they were in furtherance of the conspiracy and reasonably foreseeable.

If you think about it for a minute, you will see that this is a very potent weapon for prosecutors. It means that, if you and I agree to commit petty theft, and you kill someone in furtherance of that crime, I am equally guilty of murder even if I did not know you would kill someone or expect you to kill someone, as long as a reasonable person could have foreseen that this might happen. It means also that if 100 people agree to commit a crime — for instance money laundering — and one of the conspirators kills someone in furtherance of the common scheme, all of the other 99 conspirators can be guilty of murder, even though they did not know the murder had occurred and even though they never met the other conspirator or the victim!

The Model Penal Code recommends abolition of the Pinkerton Rule because it can make a person "accountable for thousands of additional offenses of which he was completely unaware and which he did not influence at all."[6] Many states have discarded it. But it lives on in the federal system.

What is the difference between the Pinkerton Rule and the doctrine of aiding and abetting? Both can be used to convict a person of crimes committed by another person. But they require a different *mens rea*. Aiding and abetting usually requires purpose. At a minimum, it usually requires that the defendant was subjectively aware that his accomplice would commit such an act. But Pinkerton is based on negligence. It permits a person to be guilty of a crime committed by a co-conspirator even if he did not foresee the crime, as long as a reasonable person would have foreseen it.

I say that aiding and abetting usually requires purpose because some courts follow a natural and probable consequences rule in the law of aiding and abetting. If the second crime was the natural and probable consequence of the original crime, then an accomplice to the original crime may be guilty of the second crime as well. For example, suppose we are robbing a store and you unexpectedly pull out a gun and shoot and kill the store owner. Under the traditional (and Model Penal Code) approach to aiding and abetting, I am not guilty of murder because it was not my conscious objective that you would kill, and I was not even aware that you would do so. But under the "natural and probable consequences rule," in force in some states, I would be guilty if the killing was a natural and probable consequence of the theft.

To say that a crime is a natural and probable consequence of another crime is not very different from saying that it is a reasonably foreseeable consequence of the other crime. In this respect, the Pinkerton Rule and the doctrine of accomplice liability are congruent — both require only negligence, an objective standard — but only if the state uses both the Pinkerton Rule and the "natural and probable consequences approach" to aiding and abetting.

c. The *Mens Rea* for Conspiracy.

The crime of conspiracy — as distinct from substantive crimes committed in the course of the conspiracy, or the object crime which is the objective of the conspiracy — requires two intents on the part of the conspirators. First, there must be the intent to agree. Second, there must be the intent to commit the object crime. Courts generally agree that in both senses, intent means purpose.

Notice that this means that the *mens rea* required for conspiracy can be greater than for the object crime. Take conspiracy to murder, for example. As we have seen, a person can be guilty of murder based on knowledge or recklessness. But conspiracy to murder requires an intent to murder — that is, an intent to kill. Let us revisit our plane bomb hypothetical. A and B agree to put a bomb on a plane to blow up the plane, hoping that no one will be killed but knowing that someone might be. If the bomb goes off, they can be guilty of murder, but whether the bomb goes off or not, they can not be guilty of conspiracy to murder because it was not their purpose to kill.

d. **Other Limits on Conspiracy**.

When is **abandonment** a defense to a charge of conspiracy? The common law rule is: never. Once the agreement is made (and an overt act performed, although this is not required under the common law), the conspiracy is already complete and one conspirator cannot avoid prosecution for conspiracy by abandoning the enterprise. But most courts hold that he can avoid prosecution for subsequent substantive offenses committed by the other conspirators (Pinkerton) by abandoning the conspiracy, but only if he communicates his withdrawal to the other conspirators, and sometimes only if he dissuades them from pursuing the object of the conspiracy.

The common law also requires that there be at least two persons involved in a conspiracy. This is called the plurality requirement. It does not mean that one conspirator can not be convicted if his fellow conspirator dies or escapes before he can be charged. But it does mean that if one conspirator is acquitted in one trial, the other alleged conspirator cannot be convicted in another trial. If there is a joint trial and one is acquitted and the other convicted, the conviction must be vacated.

The Model Penal Code recommends abolition of this plurality requirement. At the risk of violating Cardozo's famous aphorism that a man "cannot conspire with himself," the Code says that one can be guilty of conspiracy as long as he agrees to commit a crime, even if the person he agrees with is not guilty.

3. Conclusion: Conspiracy

Conspiracy is a controversial area of criminal law, and many have recommended that it be abolished. It has not been abolished, however, and it remains a potent weapon for prosecutors for both its procedural and substantive law advantages.

NOTES

1. This is what it means to say that conspiracy does not merge with the object crime. Attempt does merge. If I attempt to kill you and succeed, I can only be guilty of murder, not murder and attempted murder. But if I conspire with someone to kill you and do kill you, we can be guilty of both murder and conspiracy to murder. Note, however, that the Model Penal Code recommends that this possibility of double prosecution be abolished, except where the conspiracy contemplated a series of crimes and only one of them was committed.

2. This is the position of the Model Penal Code, except that the Code recommends that conspiracies to commit the worst crimes — felonies of the first degree — be punished less severely than the completed crime.

3. *Krulewitch v. U.S.*, 336 U.S. 440 (1949).

4. Like attempt, conspiracy is an inchoate crime, meaning that it is an incipient crime intended to lead to another crime.

5. The Model Penal Code recommends the abolition of the overt act requirement for conspiracies to commit the most serious crimes.

6. See Model Penal Code, Sec. 2.06, Comment at 307 (1985).

CHAPTER ELEVEN

Attempt

Consider the following hypothetical:

At 3:00 PM on June 25, Thadeus Small decides to kill Mortimer Broadstreet. At 3:30 on that same day, Thadeus loads his gun for this purpose. At 3:40, Thadeus sets out in his car for Mortimer's house. At 4:30, Thadeus arrives at the house, and waits there for Mortimer to arrive so he can shoot him to death. When Mortimer does not show up by 8:00, Thadeus goes home. Is Thadeus guilty of a crime?

Nearly all crimes occur in stages. First, the actor *thinks* about what he is going to do. Then, he *prepares* to commit the crime. Then he *begins* to commit it. Finally, he *commits* it.

We have already seen that criminal law does not punish the first stage: it is not a crime to think evil thoughts. And, of course, we do punish the final stage — the commission of the crime. But what if we are in the middle? What if you have gone beyond thinking but have not completed the crime?

When conduct is made criminal in this intermediate stage, we call it an inchoate crime. We have already seen an example of an inchoate crime — conspiracy. And we made reference to another one, solicitation. Now, we are going to examine a third inchoate crime: attempt.

Attempt differs from conspiracy in three important ways. First, conspiracy generally requires two or more people, but attempt does not. Second, conspiracy can occur earlier than attempt because the overt act sometimes required for conspiracy can be an innocent act that falls far short of an attempt. Third, unlike conspiracy, there is no stacking of charges with attempt; if I attempt to kill you and do kill you, I can be charged only with murder, not with murder and attempted murder. Put differently, a person cannot be convicted of both a completed offense and an attempt to commit it.

1. How and Why is Attempt Punished?

The crime of attempt[1] is a relatively new one in Anglo-American legal history. According to the authoritative *History of English Law* by Pollock and Maitland, old English law proceeded on the assumption that "an attempt to do harm is no offense."[2] That is why it is sometimes said that, in those days, a "miss was as good as a mile."

In time, the English courts began to work out crimes of attempted treason and attempted subversion of justice, as in cases where people tried to bribe the king's judges. The infamous Court of Star Chamber, which we saw in the history of conspiracy, played a key role in formulating and enforcing these crimes. But neither Star Chamber nor Parliament got around to promulgating a general law of attempt until well into the eighteenth century.

In America today, most states have a general attempt statute, which applies to an attempt to commit any felony or misdemeanor. Many states also have specific statutes making it a crime to attempt specific other crimes.

An argument can be made that we should not punish attempts at all. After all, in the hypothetical at the start of this chapter, what harm did Thadeus's actions do? Suppose Thadeus had fired a gun through the window of Mortimer's home while Mortimer was inside asleep, but had missed him and the police had captured Thadeus before Mortimer even knew what happened? What harm did Thadeus cause? Even if Thadeus fired his gun straight at Mortimer and missed and then was caught, is

there any harm that cannot be taken care of by another crime —
for example, assault or battery?

There is, of course, a response to this argument. You could say
that harm should be more broadly defined. A person, in this view,
does cause harm if he shoots at someone while they are asleep,
even if the victim never hears the shot and it misses. Then too, it
is said that punishing attempts helps law enforcement by permitting the police to prevent crimes before they cause irreparable
harm. Like conspiracy, attempt provides a way to reach criminality early on. Finally, an attempt conviction is based on the
assumption that the defendant is dangerous because he is dis-
posed to try again; he represents, in other words, a continuing
danger to the victim and/or to the society at large.

Most states punish attempt less severely than the completed
crime. Should they punish it the same? Note that the Model Penal
Code recommends punishment of attempt at the same level as the
object crime, as with conspiracy.

2. Attempt: Mens Rea

Attempt is what the common law calls a specific intent crime.
This means that, in order to be guilty of an attempt, you must
intend to do the action that constitutes the attempt *and* you must
also intend the object crime.

This is relatively straightforward when the object crime is a
conduct crime — a crime for which the *actus reus* is merely
conduct and result is not required. For example, say that you are
drunk and you get behind the wheel of a car and start the motor.
Right then, you are guilty of attempted drunk driving.

But suppose the crime is a **result** crime, like criminal homicide. For attempted murder, you must intend to kill. Notice that
this means that the *mens rea* for attempted murder is *greater* than
for murder. If attempted murder is punished less severely than
murder, and it is practically everywhere, and never more severely, why do we make the *mens rea* for attempted murder
greater than for murder?

Consider the following hypotheticals:

    1) A kills B with intent to kill.

    2) A kills B with intent to grievously injure B.

3) A kills B with a reckless disregard for B's life.

Now change the hypotheticals to imagine that B does not die. Is A guilty of attempted murder? Suppose a drunken man drives 80 mph on the wrong side of the highway, hitting a pedestrian but not killing him. Would that be attempted murder?

Consider the following case:

People v. Gentry
Appellate Court of Illinois, First District, 1987

Stanley Gentry was convicted of attempted murder . . . .

On December 13, 1983, Gentry and Ruby Hill, Gentry's girlfriend, were in the apartment they shared [and] . . . began to argue. During the argument, Gentry spilled gasoline on Hill, and the gasoline . . . ignited. Gentry was able to smother the flames with a coat, but only after Hill had been severely burned . . . .

Hill testified . . . that [they] had been drinking [heavily] . . . . [She also testified that the] gasoline ignited only after she had gone near the stove in the kitchen . . . .

[The trial judge permitted the jury to convict Gentry of attempted murder if he] acted with knowledge that his conduct created a strong probability of death or serious bodily harm to Hill, even if the jury believed Gentry did not act with specific intent to kill. [This was erroneous.]

We reverse defendant's conviction and sentence.

Suppose that the facts had showed that Gentry had thrown a match near Hill after he doused her with gasoline. Could he be guilty of attempted murder if the state proved that he did this to teach her a lesson, knowing that there was a high probability that she would burn to death? What would the Model Penal Code say?

Is it possible to attempt other degrees of criminal homicide? What about attempted voluntary manslaughter? Attempted involuntary manslaughter? Attempted felony murder? What mental state should be required for each of these?

Suppose a pharmacist accidentally puts the wrong label on a drug. Mislabeling a drug is a strict liability felony. A child takes the drug and nearly dies. Is the pharmacist guilty of attempted felony murder? Suppose a man is robbing a shoe store. In the course of the robbery, the owner of the store accidentally bumps into his gun, causing it to go off, almost hitting and killing someone. Is this attempted felony murder? Would it be attempted felony murder as soon as the felony began?

Many states do permit a charge of attempted voluntary manslaughter, on the theory that such a crime is an intentional killing. But few permit attempted involuntary manslaughter, and few permit attempted felony murder, although some do permit the latter. Do you see why?

Suppose A starts to have sex with B, believing B is 20 years old. When A finds out B is only 18, A stops. Is A guilty of attempted statutory rape? If A had continued with the act, he would be guilty, even if he did not find out her true age, because, in most states, statutory rape is a strict liability offense with respect to the woman's age. No *mens rea* is required for this *attendant circumstance*. But what *mens rea* should be required for attempted statutory rape? If attempt generally requires an *intent* to commit the object offense, does this mean that A is not guilty unless he intended to have sex with a girl under the age of consent or knew that she was under age? Or does strict liability also apply to the attempt?

3. Attempt: Actus Reus

The most difficult question in the law of attempt is determining when mere preparation ends and the attempt begins. Several different tests have been formulated to ascertain this line. The test one uses is largely determined by whether one is an objectivist or a subjectivist with respect to such things.

An **objectivist** in the law of attempt believes that a court should only punish a person for actions which are objectively criminal in themselves. Otherwise, we may punish people just for thinking bad thoughts.

Subjectivists say that if the court has evidence of the defendant's mental state (from a confession, for example), the court should convict the defendant of an attempt if he does any act, no matter whether it is criminal or not and no matter how apparently innocuous it is, as long as it corroborates the criminal intent. Subjectivists worry that the objectivist approach would require police to wait until the harm is already done.

Consider the following hypothetical to illustrate this issue:

Suppose A, intending to kill B, puts what he thinks is arsenic in B's tea. In fact, it is not arsenic, but icing sugar. Is A guilty of attempted murder?

If we have a confession by A or some other evidence that he intended to kill B, a subjectivist would say that A is guilty, because his culpable mental state is corroborated by his action.

But an objectivist would say that A is not guilty because his action, pouring sugar into tea, is not objectively criminal or dangerous. By itself, it does not prove that A intended to kill B. In light of these two general perspectives, consider the following tests of when an attempt begins:

a. **The Last Proximate Act Test**.

Courts used to employ the last proximate act test. This meant that one was not guilty of an attempt unless one did the very last thing one could do, and the intended harm did not occur. For instance, if I point a gun at your head and announce that I am going to kill you immediately, this is not attempted murder under this approach unless I actually pull the trigger. Few if any courts today adopt this approach.

b. **The *Res Ipsa Loquitor* or Unequivocality Approach**.

Under this approach, popular with objectivists, there is no attempt unless the defendant performs some act which "speaks for itself" — in other words, an act which, by itself, shows the intended guilty end. If the act is ambiguous (equivocal), there is no attempt.

This approach asks the court to view the defendant's acts as if it were watching a silent movie. Apart from any evidence of defendant's motives or intent, apart from any confessions, do the acts themselves manifest a criminal purpose? Many commentators have criticized this approach, saying it amounts to the last proximate act in practice because it is often only when the defendant does the last proximate act that his action clearly proclaims his guilty purpose.

c. **The Model-Penal-Code Approach**.

The Model Penal Code takes a subjectivist approach to attempt. The Code recommends that a person be guilty of attempt as long as he takes a substantial step which corroborates the actor's intent. The Code does not require that the actor's conduct speak for itself, as the *Res Ipsa Loquitor* test would have it. This approach is taken now by the majority of states, in one form or another.

4. Alternatives to Attempt

One purpose of the law of attempt is to punish criminal behavior before it causes irreparable harm. But if we define an attempt to require close proximity to the completed crime, the police may be unable to arrest the culprit until the harm has already been done. For instance, suppose A breaks into B's house intending to rob him. If the police stop A just as he enters, has he committed attempted larceny? Not if we use the last proximate act rule. Possibly not if we use the *Res Ipsa Loquitor* test, since we do not know for sure what A's intent is yet. Even if we use substantial step, the result is not absolutely certain.

For this reason, legislatures have, over the years, developed other anticipatory crimes which can occur before an attempt occurs. For instance, in the example above, even if A is not guilty of attempted larceny, he would be guilty of burglary. Assault is another anticipatory offense. If I point a gun at you and threaten to kill you, I might not be guilty of attempted murder, but I might well be guilty of assault.

Can one be charged with attempted assault or attempted burglary? Suppose A was arrested before he broke in. Would this be attempted burglary?

The law of attempt and conspiracy shows us that actions can be criminal long before the criminal's intended object is realized. Are there also circumstances where the object *is* realized, but the defendant is not guilty? This raises the issue of defenses — an important topic to which we now turn.

NOTES

1. Like conspiracy and aiding and abetting, attempt is not really a crime by itself. One must speak of attempted murder or attempted rape or attempted burglary, and so on.

2. Frederick Pollock and Frederick William Maitland, *History of English Law Before the Time of Edward I* (2nd edit., 1903), p. 508, n. 4, cited in LaFave and Scott, *Criminal Law*, p. 495, n.2.

CHAPTER TWELVE

Defenses

Suppose that Vladimir Snoopington shoots and kills Estelle Gates. Charged with murder, Vladimir defends by saying that:

a. when he shot at Gates, he thought her body was a tree rather than a human being.

b. he was unconscious when he shot Gates.

c. he did not shoot Gates and was no where near the scene of the crime when the shooting took place.

In common parlance, we call each of these arguments a "defense." But, in law, none of these is properly speaking a defense. All three of these claims dispute an important aspect of the prosecution's case in chief:

a. the argument in a. claims lack of *mens rea*;

b. the argument in b. and c. claims lack of *actus reus* (in situation 2 because the defendant did not do a voluntary act; in situation 3, because defendant was not the one who acted).

A true defense is one which exculpates the defendant even though the prosecution has proved every element of the crime beyond reasonable doubt. Thus, although the defendant would certainly be able to raise all three of these claims in any court, we should not call them true defenses.

Why does it matter whether we call them true defenses or not?

If they are not true defenses — if they are *elements of the crime* — the burden of proof must be on the prosecution. The defense may have the *burden of production* — the burden of raising the issue first. But once the defense raises the issue, the *burden of persuasion* on all elements of the crime is left to the prosecution, and the prosecution must always meet this burden by a standard of proof beyond reasonable doubt. In other words, in the hypothetical above, once Vladimir introduced some evidence to show that he did not know he was shooting at a human body (a mistake of fact) or that he was unconscious or had an alibi, it would be up to the state to prove, beyond a reasonable doubt, that he *did* know he was shooting a human body, or that he *was* conscious or did *not* have an alibi.

For true defenses, however, the defense *may* be asked to bear the burden of both production *and* persuasion. In other words, these defenses say that, even though the state may have proved every element of the crime beyond reasonable doubt, the defendant is still not guilty.

There are essentially **four types of true defenses**:

a. **Justification defenses**, as we have seen, pertain to behavior which, although otherwise criminal, is socially acceptable and even praiseworthy under the circumstances. Killing in self-defense is a justification defense.

b. **Excuse defenses**, as we have also seen, excuse the actor rather than the act. Insanity is an excuse defense.

c. **Specialized defenses** pertain only to certain crimes in special ways.[1] Impossibility and abandonment may be defenses to attempt, for instance.

d. Finally there are what some lawyers call **extrinsic defenses**, which serve a public policy goal that is not directly related to the social harm of the act or the defendant's blame-worthiness. Examples include a defense that the statute of limitations has run out or that the defendant has diplomatic immunity.

1. Specialized Defenses to Attempt

a. **Impossibility**.

Suppose that A puts his hand in B's pocket, intending to steal B's wallet. But the pocket is empty. Suppose that C smokes what he believes is marijuana, but in fact it is a form of tobacco, which it is legal to smoke. Suppose that D fires a gun into E's house intending to kill E, but D does not kill E because the gun, unknown to D, is not loaded, or because E is not at home, or because the bullet hits E when E is already dead. Are A, C, and D guilty of attempted larceny (pick-pocketing), attempted marijuana smoking, and attempted murder, respectively? Or do any of these defendants have a defense that what they were trying to do was impossible?

More has been written about the complex defense of impossibility than practically any other area of criminal law. The general common law rule is that factual impossibility is not a defense, but legal impossibility is. But what is the difference between factual impossibility and legal impossibility? It is not always easy to see any difference.

Factual impossibility means that what the defendant was trying to do was a crime, but it was not possible for him to do it because of some fact of which he was not aware. Examples of factual impossibility include firing an unloaded gun, trying to give a person AIDS by spitting at them, and picking an empty pocket.

Courts are not sympathetic to such claims, and practically any court would convict a defendant in such cases (of attempted murder in the first two situations, and attempted larceny in the third). In all these cases, if the facts had been as the defendant supposed them to be, there would have been a crime. Moreover, there is an *actus reus*, there is *mens rea*, and the defendant's action demonstrates his dangerousness.

When we come to legal impossibility, it is more proper to distinguish between pure legal impossibility and a sort of "hybrid" legal impossibility and factual impossibility. Pure legal impossibility is *always* a defense. Many courts think that *hybrid legal impossibility* is indistinguishable from factual impossibility, and thus not a valid defense.

With pure legal impossibility, what the defendant is trying to do is not a crime at all. For example, suppose A tries to buy beer on a Sunday in a state where it is perfectly legal to buy beer on Sunday. No court will convict A of attempted purchase of beer on Sunday. There is no such crime!

Consider a more difficult case. Suppose defendant takes a check made out to him in the amount of $2.50 and alters the numerical part of the check to read $12.50. He does not alter the written part of the check, which still reads "two and 50/100 dollars." Check forgery requires alteration of a material part of the check. The numerical part of the check is not material, since banks, when confronted with a discrepancy between the numerical portion and the written portion of the check, will honor the latter. The defendant is thus not guilty of check forgery. Can he be charged with attempted check forgery?

The Mississippi Supreme Court said no in the case of *Wilson v. State* back in 1905. Even though Wilson intended to forge the check the court said he did not commit attempted forgery because the specific thing he was trying to do — alter the numerical part of the check and thereby cash more money for himself than he was entitled to — would not constitute forgery.

Practically all courts today would agree with the decision in *Wilson*. If you try to do something that is not a crime, they say, you cannot be convicted of an attempt to commit a crime. Wilson was attempting to forge a check by altering only the numerical part of it. There is no such thing as forgery by altering the numerical part of the check only. Therefore, he cannot be guilty of attempted forgery.

Another way of looking at the *Wilson* case is that Wilson's only error was that he did not know the rule of law — that the numerical part of the check is legally immaterial. That is why, strictly speaking, he has a defense of pure legal impossibility.

But suppose a defendant receives what he thinks are stolen goods, but they are not stolen. A court in *People v. Jaffe* said he could not be convicted of attempting to commit the crime of knowing receipt of stolen goods because the goods were not stolen. Even if he had completed his action, he would not be guilty of any crime, so he has a defense of pure legal impossibility.

But is the case of *Jaffe* really indistinguishable from *Wilson*? In *Wilson*, there was only an error of law. But in *Jaffe*, the defendant is mistaken as to a particular fact — that the goods are not stolen. If the facts had been as he believed them to be —if, in other words, the goods *were* stolen — then Jaffe *would* be guilty of a crime. This is why many commentators say that the *Jaffe* case, unlike *Wilson*, is a hybrid legal and factual impossibility situation, and thus one in which no defense need be available.

Consider again the defendant who shoots at a corpse, believing it to be a live human being. As in *Jaffe*, if the *facts* had

been as he believed them to be — if the body had been alive —
he would be guilty of murder. Thus, he can be guilty of
attempted murder, some courts say. Other courts say that, since
shooting a corpse is not a crime, he cannot be guilty of attempted
murder, any more than Jaffe could be guilty of attempting to
receive stolen goods when they were not stolen.

Some courts today continue to affirm the *Jaffe* precedent,
and thus hold that a defendant cannot be guilty of attempted
receipt of stolen property if, unknown to him, the goods are not
stolen, or of attempting to bribe a juror if the person he offers
money to is not a juror, or of attempted murder if he shoots at
a corpse. Other courts reject this view, and declare that defendants in such cases *can* be guilty of attempt.

The latter approach is more typical of modern statutory
solutions to the problem of impossibility. Most modern state
criminal codes thus follow the lead of the Model Penal Code in
abolishing the defense of impossibility except in two special
circumstances: 1) pure legal impossibility, where even if the *facts*
had been exactly as the defendant believed them to be, he would
still not be guilty of any crime because what he was trying to do
was not a crime at all (e.g., buying beer in a state where such
purchase is legal) and 2) inherently impossible attempts (e.g.,
trying to kill someone with a feather).[2]

b. **Abandonment**.

Suppose that Charles rents a room in an apartment building
overlooking Eaton Square so he can shoot Matilda as she walks
through the square on her way to work. Charles brings his gun
to the apartment and looks for Matilda each day, but she does
not show up. After a week of waiting, Charles decides that
killing Matilda is a bad idea, so he goes home. Has Charles
committed attempted murder of Matilda?

There are two ways to look at this issue. The first way,
discussed in the previous chapter on attempts, is to ask whether
the defendant's actions were close enough to the completed
crime to constitute an attempt. Here, the unequivocality test or
the substantial step (MPC) test would be relevant.

But suppose we conclude that he did come close enough to
the crime to constitute an attempt. Can he nevertheless be
acquitted of attempted murder on the grounds of abandonment?

Abandonment is not a defense to most crimes. If you offer

to give back the goods you have stolen and renounce your life of crime, this is no defense to the crime of larceny, for instance. But some courts do allow abandonment as a defense to attempted crimes, provided that the abandonment was voluntary and complete. In other words, a defendant is not entitled to a defense of abandonment if the reason he gave up the scheme was because he was afraid the police would catch him or because he postponed the crime until a better day or because the victim resisted with unexpected force. There must be a complete, voluntary change of heart for abandonment to be applicable. The Model Penal Code recognizes a defense of abandonment to attempt charges in situations like this, and many states do too.

Suppose that Charles, in our hypothetical above, had shot at Matilda and missed, or shot her and not killed her, and *then* had given up his scheme to murder her. Few if any courts would say he has a defense of abandonment, even if his decision is based on a voluntary and complete change of heart. In other words, even where the defense of abandonment is available, it lasts only a certain period of time — until sufficient "harm" has been done.

2. Hypothetical Case.

Joe Winters, a 20-year-old college student, has lived in Washington, DC his entire life. On several occasions, he has been the victim of muggings on the streets of DC. Twice he was badly beaten by muggers, once so seriously that he almost died.

Sometime during his senior year at college, Winters begins to believe that God wants him to save DC from muggers. He fancies himself a vigilante hero, protecting women and children from the menace of criminals on the streets.

Winters also has recurring dreams. In one dream, he is honored by a ticker-tape parade down Pennsylvania Avenue and decorated by the President at the White House; he even dreams of making a speech about the dangers of mugging before a Joint Session of Congress. In another dream, Winters imagines that he is riding on the subway when a vicious looking old man comes up to him, pulls out a knife, and starts stabbing him. Terrified by this nightmare, Winters goes out and buys a gun.

Late one night, Winters gets on the DC Metro (subway) at the Foggy Bottom station, bound for Capitol South. Just as the train is pulling out of the Metro Center stop, an old man, who had been sitting opposite Winters in the subway car, gets up, walks up to Winters, and asks him for a match. The old man puts his hand in his pocket, reaching for a cigarette. Winters looks at his face and suddenly he sees the face of the old man in his nightmare. Shouting, "He's got a knife!" Winters jumps up, pulls the gun out of his own pocket, and fires it into the old man's chest, killing him. Winters then fires his gun wildly, killing the three other people who are in the subway car as they scream and race to the exit. Then Winters flees.

Some time later, Winters is captured and charged with murder. He defends by pleading self-defense and insanity. You are the judge. How do you rule on Winters' claim?

3. Self-Defense

a. **Introduction.**

The principles of self-defense as a justification in criminal law are very similar to those which provide a defense to intentional torts: in general, a person does not commit a crime if he uses a reasonable and proportionate amount of force against another person whom he reasonably believes is about to injure or kill him.

In criminal law, the defense of self-defense usually arises in one of two contexts. First, the defense can arise in prosecutions for criminal homicide (including murder and manslaughter), attempted murder, or assault with intent to kill. In these situations, the defendant claims that he used *deadly* force in self-defense. Second, the defense can arise in prosecutions for assault or battery. In these situations, the defendant claims that he used *non-deadly* force in self-defense.

Can a claim of self-defense be raised for other crimes as well? Suppose that A draws a knife to stab B to death. B, escaping from A, takes A's car to make his getaway. Is B guilty of larceny? No, but not because of self-defense. The law will usually call that a defense of necessity — a separate claim.

The most interesting cases of self-defense are of the first type — those that arise in homicide prosecutions. For this reason, our emphasis in this section will be on when the use of deadly force is justifiable self-defense.

b. **Self-Defense by Deadly Force: Rationale of the Defense**.

It is sometimes said that the law allows a person to kill in self-defense because, confronted with an imminent threat to life from another person, any reasonable person would kill. But it is questionable whether the defense is really based on reason. After all, a person in such a situation has little luxury to be reasonable. As Holmes said, "detached reflection cannot be demanded in the presence of an uplifted knife." Moreover, animals, it has been said, often kill in self-defense by instinct, and animals do not reason.

Instead of being a testament to human reason, then, the law of self-defense appears to be an acknowledgment of what Blackstone once called the "primary law of nature." The common law, Blackstone went on, "respects the passions of the human mind." Chief among those passions is the conviction, deeply rooted in the human soul, that choosing your life over that of a deadly adversary is entirely acceptable.

c. **What is Deadly Force?**

Deadly force is usually defined as "force likely to cause death or grievous bodily injury." More precisely, it is force which is either inflicted with the *intent* to cause death or serious injury or which is inflicted with *knowledge* that it may very well cause death or serious bodily injury. Merely *threatening* to kill or cause serious bodily harm is not using deadly force. Thus, some courts have said, a person may be justified in pointing a gun at his attacker (using non-deadly force) when he would not be justified in firing the gun (using deadly force). Put differently, if you are justified in using deadly force, you are always justified in using non-deadly force. But if you are justified in using non-deadly force, you are not always justified in using deadly force.

d. **The Elements of Self-Defense**.

First, the defendant must **honestly and reasonably believe** in the necessity of using deadly force to repel the attack. It does not matter if the belief is wrong, as long as it is reasonable. For instance, suppose in the hypothetical about Winters and the subway killing, that the old man had told Winters the day before that he was going to kill him. Winters would be able to claim he acted in self-defense if he killed the old man as he reached his hand in his pocket, even if in fact the old man was only reaching for a cigarette, as long as a reasonable person would think — given the previous threat and given the act of reaching in the pocket — that the old man was about to inflict a deadly attack.

On the other hand, if Winters was *drunk* and, because of his intoxication, erroneously thought that the old man was about to attack him, courts will not say he was acting in self-defense. The standard is that of the reasonable sober man, not the reasonable drunk one. Beyond being sober, however, the reasonable man may have some of the characteristics of the accused — especially physical characteristics like size, age, sex, and strength.

For instance, suppose an elderly 5'2" woman opens her front door and finds a 6'8" man whom she knows has just been in a mental institution standing there. When the man says something unintelligible, the woman screams and, thinking he is about to attack her, stabs him with a kitchen knife, killing him. The court might very well say that the standard against which to measure her actions is that of a reasonable woman of that age and height, when confronted with a man of that size and background. Other factors — including the number of potential assailants and past violent conduct known to the defendant — may be taken into account in assessing the "reasonableness" of the defendant's perception.

The Model Penal Code recommends that an honest but unreasonable belief in the necessity of self-defense be sufficient, but few courts accept this. Thus, in the Winters hypothetical, the Model Penal Code would allow Winters to plead self-defense if he honestly believed the old man was about to kill him, even if no reasonable person would have believed that.[3] Under the law of most states, however, Winters would have no claim of self-defense if his belief, however honest, was unreasonable.

Practically all jurisdictions insist that the defendant *actually* believed in the necessity to act in self-defense at the time of the attack. If the defendant was not aware of the threat, he did not kill in self-defense.

The second requirement for use of deadly force in self-defense is that the threatened attack be **imminent**. The rationale for this requirement is that if the threatened harm could happen hours or even days later, there is time for the intended victim to call the police or use other legal avenues rather than killing. But what if the intended victim is not in a position to use any of those legal avenues? For instance, suppose a kidnapper captures A and holds him at knife-point, telling him he is going to kill him in a week's time. One morning, six days before the expected attack, A sees his chance and grabs the kidnapper's gun and shoots him to death. Many courts would say that A acted in self-defense, because the threatened harm might not have been avoided if A waited until the last minute — until the attack was literally "imminent."

The Model Penal Code gets around this problem by substituting the phrase "immediately necessary on the present occasion" for the common law term "imminent." Thus a physically-abused wife who kills her husband when he tells her he is going out to look for a knife to stab her to death can claim self-defense, under the Model Penal Code, because if she waited until he returned with the knife, it might be too late.

But what if she kills him while he is asleep? Can she claim self-defense then? These are the so-called "hard cases," to which the "battered woman's syndrome" seems particularly relevant.

Evidence of that syndrome is often introduced to help the jury understand why the woman did not just leave home, and most courts accept that it is relevant in assessing the credibility of her claims that she was in fear of her life. The dispute about the use of such expert testimony, however, largely turns on whether the evidence can also be used to help the jury decide the *reasonableness* of the woman's perceptions. Many commentators say yes. In effect, they say, the standard in such a case should be that of the reasonable battered woman. Many courts, however, say no, insisting that reasonableness is an issue for the jury, not for experts. No jury needs an expert to tell them what is reasonable, courts sometimes say.

The third requirement for the use of deadly force in self-defense is that the attack you are responding to must be **unlawful**, or rather that the defendant must reasonably *think* it is unlawful. You cannot lawfully kill in response to known lawful force or force to which you have consented.

Suppose you are crossing the street and an insane person suddenly jumps out of a car and attacks you with a knife. In an effort to save yourself, you push him into an oncoming car, killing him. Will the law say you did not act in self-defense because the insane person was not committing a crime (since he could not be punished because of his insanity)? Of course not! An *excused* act is still an unlawful act for these purposes. The same would apply if you were to be attacked by a child or an intoxicated person or a drug addict.

Special problems sometimes arise when a person uses force to resist an unlawful arrest. In most states, the arrested person is justified in using *non-deadly* force in such situations. If he uses deadly force and kills, many states, following the common law approach, will reduce the crime from murder to voluntary manslaughter, on the theory that an unlawful arrest is the sort of provocation which the common law recognizes as legally sufficient. But many commentators take the view that a person who uses force to resist an unlawful arrest should have no defense at all, at least when the person knows that the person arresting him is a police officer. To hold otherwise, they say, is to encourage violent responses to unlawful police actions, rather than legal ones. The Model Penal Code adopts this view, although the arrestee is permitted to use force if he believes the police officer is using more force than necessary to effect the unlawful arrest.

A fourth requirement for the use of deadly force in self-defense is that your response must be **proportional** to the threatened attack. You are not justified in using *deadly* force unless you reasonably believe your attacker is about to kill you or seriously injure you *and* that the only way you can avoid this result is to use deadly force against him. If you are involved in a traffic accident on the freeway and the driver of the car with which you have collided walks up to you and appears to be about to punch you in the nose, you cannot legally push him into a lane of traffic (use deadly force) even if there is no way to avoid the punch except to do this. On the other hand, if you reasonably fear that he is about to beat you up very badly, you could take such a step if necessary to avert the life-threatening injury.

Suppose you do not fear your attacker will *kill* you. Suppose, instead, you fear imminent robbery or rape, or another violent felony. Can you then kill in self-defense? Modern state statutes, following the lead of the Model Penal Code, typically permit killing in such circumstances. The Model Code also includes kidnapping as a crime you can kill to prevent, but this seems to depend on kidnapping being defined as a crime of violence — not when kidnapping is used to apply to a divorced wife or husband taking possession of children to which he or she is not entitled.

Suppose you reasonably believe someone is about to perpetrate one of these violent felonies on someone else. Can you kill in "defense of another"? Under the old common law, you could only do so if the apparent victim was a blood relative or spouse or someone to whom you owed a duty (recall the law on omissions). Now, courts rarely impose such requirements. According to most modern state codes, it is legal to kill in defense of a stranger who is being raped by force or threatened with murder in front of your eyes.

But what if your belief that the stranger is in dire peril is wrong? Suppose you see two men apparently beating up a younger man on the street. You rush to the young man's aid, killing the two older men. Then you discover that the two men were undercover police officers making a lawful arrest. Can you claim a defense?

Some courts adopt the rule that you "stand in the shoes of the victim." If the young man in this incident would not have a claim of self-defense — and, presumably, he would not have, since the police were making a lawful arrest — then you do not either. Other courts take the view that, as long as your belief in the necessity to rescue was *reasonable*, it does not matter that the apparent "victim" had no such valid claim.

Closely related to these issues is the rule that you cannot claim you acted in self-defense if you were the **aggressor** in the conflict. This, then, may be taken as the fifth element in the law of self-defense by deadly force: "one cannot support a claim of self-defense by a self-generated necessity to kill."[4]

You do not have to commit an assault or battery to be the aggressor. A threat, or indeed any act reasonably calculated to produce a forcible response, may be sufficient. On the other hand, you are never "the aggressor" if your act is lawful. An aggressor, then, is one who takes or threatens some unlawful action likely to incite another to violence.

There are two situations in which a person who *is* the aggressor can claim he killed in self-defense, however. Suppose that Gertrude slaps William across the face. Enraged, William pulls out a knife and tries to stab Gertrude. Gertrude shoots William to death.

Gertrude was the first aggressor. Her slap, presumably, was unlawful (a misdemeanor) and likely to produce a forcible response of some kind. But William's response was so disproportionate to the slap that, in effect, William became the new aggressor. Under these circumstances, Gertrude was justified in killing William. If Gertrude had been shooting at William instead of slapping him, and William had responded with the knife, Gertrude would not be able to assert that she acted in self-defense when she killed William because his action was perfectly legal — he was defending himself against her murderous attack.

The second situation in which an aggressor can claim self-defense is where the aggressor *withdraws* from the fray. If you punch someone in a bar and then go home and your victim follows you home and beats you up en route, that is not self-defense (to a charge of assault and battery) on his part. Courts usually require that the withdrawing aggressor make known his intentions to withdraw to the victim. What if any reasonable person would see that the aggressor is withdrawing but the defendant cannot see this because he is so dazed by the attack?

Suppose it is not the aggressor but the victim who has an opportunity to withdraw. What if, instead of fighting back, the victim could run away? Is it self-defense if he stands his ground and kills?

On the one hand, the law recognizes a strong policy interest in avoiding unnecessary violence. On the other hand, there is a strong policy against forcing someone to play the coward.

Courts never require a defendant to retreat before using *non-deadly* force. Most courts also do *not* require the defendant to retreat before using *deadly* force. A substantial minority of states, however, hold that a person must retreat before using deadly force, if he can retreat in complete safety. Those states which take this view nearly always make an exception for one's own home or office: there is no duty to retreat from one's own home (the so-called "castle" exception) or office, although there may be a duty to retreat even from the home if the assailant is a co-occupant.[5]

The Model Penal Code recommends the minority view on the retreat issue: a person may not use deadly force against another if he knows he can retreat in complete safety. The Code specifies that "the actor is not obliged to retreat from his dwelling or place of work, unless he was the initial agressor or is assailed in his place of work by another person whose place of work the actor knows it to be."

e. "Imperfect" Self-Defense.

We have seen that most states require the defendant's belief in the necessity to use deadly force be *reasonable* in order for him to claim he killed in self-defense. What if the defendant's belief was not reasonable? Suppose a jury concludes that Winters, in the subway hypothetical, honestly believed the old man was about to attack him, but a reasonable person would not have believed that. Or suppose the jury says that a reasonable person would have believed the old man was about to make a *non-deadly* attack on him, thus making Winters' *deadly* response unreasonable. What kind of crime should Winters be guilty of?

There are a number of alternatives in such situations. The traditional common law rule, still apparently followed by some states, is that, if the defendant's response is not reasonable, his self-defense claim just gets wiped out. Since he did kill intentionally (and has no defense of self-defense), he is guilty of murder. Courts taking this view would find Winters guilty of murder of the old man on the subway.

A second approach is to say that, although the unreasonableness of defendant's response precludes a complete defense, the fact that he *thought* he was acting in legitimate self-defense means the crime should be mitigated to some kind of manslaughter. Some courts call it voluntary manslaughter, on the theory that defendant was in a state of passion when he acted, but others say it cannot be voluntary manslaughter because a reasonable person would not have been provoked since a reasonable person would have known there was no threat. Other courts call it involuntary manslaughter, reasoning that, although the killing was intentional (most killings that constitute involuntary manslaughter are unintentional, as we have seen), still the defendant intended to kill only in self-defense.

The Model Penal Code solution to this issue is the "lowest common denominator" approach. The Code, as we have seen, allows a defendant to plead self-defense if he had an honest belief in the necessity of using deadly force, even if that belief was totally unreasonable. But, the code also provides that such a defense is unavailable in any prosecution for which reckless-ness or negligence provides the basis for criminality.

For example, suppose that a court finds that Winters was negligent in his response to the old man. In other words, Winters did not know there was a big risk that the old man was not really attacking him, but a reasonable person would have known of such a risk. The Model Penal Code would say that Winters can plead self-defense to a charge of *murder*, or even *manslaughter*, since, under the Code, murder and manslaughter require at least recklessness (a subjective awareness of the risk). But the Code would say that Winters would have *no defense* to a charge of *negligent homicide*, a crime for which negligence (objective standard) is all that is required. Put differently, Winters would be guilty of negligent homicide because negli-gence is the *lowest* mental state that has been proved with respect to his killing. He intended to kill, but he was only negligent about the necessity of killing. So, the Code says he is guilty only of negligent homicide.

Notice that states following the strict common law rule would say that Winters is guilty of *murder* in such a situation. He intended to kill. He has no claim of self-defense because he did not respond reasonably. There is no legally sufficient provoca-tion because a reasonable person would not have been tempted to kill. Thus, defendant is guilty of murder. It thus makes a *big* difference whether one uses the common law or Model Penal Code approaches to imperfect self-defense.

Suppose that Winters had not, in fact, killed the old man on the subway, but had only wounded him with his gunshot. Could Winters be guilty of attempted murder? The common law approach would say yes, because he has no claim of self-defense and, since he did try to kill the old man, he is guilty of attempted murder.

What about under the Code? Remember that the Code specifies that honest but unreasonable or reckless self-defense is a justification for any crime that requires intent to kill, although it is not a defense to a crime requiring only reckless-ness or negligence. But can attempted murder be proved through recklessness or negligence? No. As we have seen, attempted murder — like all attempt crimes — requires *intent*. Thus, under the Model Penal Code, Winters could *not* be guilty of attempted murder even if he was reckless in his belief that the old man was about to attack him because his intent was only to kill in self-defense.

In the *Goetz* case, the New York Court of Appeals rejected the model penal code approach to imperfect self-defense, ruling that Goetz *could* be convicted of attempted murder if he honestly but unreasonably believed he needed to use deadly force to save himself when confronted by four youths on a New York subway in 1984.

f. **Risk to Innocent Bystanders**.

Another problem closely related to imperfect self-defense comes up when innocent bystanders are killed in a self defensive killing. For example, suppose that Winters really did kill the old man in self-defense in the subway hypothetical. He also killed several other people on the subway by accident. What crime would he be guilty of for their deaths?

The general rule in this area seems to be that if you are acting in lawful self-defense and, through no fault of your own, you accidentally kill an innocent third party, there is no crime. If I start choking you, and you pull out a gun and shoot me, and the bullet goes through my body and hits and kills another innocent person, you are not guilty of any crime for that person's death. On the other hand, if you were *reckless* about the life of the other person — if, like Winters, you fired your gun wildly — and you hit and killed an innocent person, you could well be guilty of manslaughter (of the reckless involuntary manslaughter type) for their death.

g. **"Self-Defense" of Property**.

Suppose a mugger grabs your wallet in a crowd and starts to abscond with it. Can you pull out a gun and shoot the mugger dead as he flees to get your wallet back? Suppose a burglar breaks into your house to steal your television set. Can you stab the burglar to death with a steak knife?

The defense of *property* must be distinguished from the defense of *habitation*. Under certain circumstances, a person is legally justified in using non-deadly force to protect his property, real or personal, from imminent dispossession by another, or to regain that property immediately after another has dispossessed him of it. Under certain circumstances, a person is legally justified in using non-deadly or even deadly force to protect his home from an unlawful intruder. The difference is that, while deadly force is sometimes justified to protect the home, it is never justified to protect property.

The reason for this distinction is that the law favors human life over protection of property. It prefers people to resolve property disputes by non-violent means. But it does allow a person to use non-deadly force if he is in possession of an item of property, against a person who reasonably appears to threaten imminent dispossession of that property, but only so much force (and never deadly force) as is necessary to protect the property.

Notice that you do not have to have *title* to the property to have a right to use non-deadly force to protect it. As long as you have rightful *possession* of the property, that is enough. Thus, for example, a tenant may, under some circumstances, use non-deadly force to prevent a landlord from unlawfully evicting him from the premises.

Use of deadly force is never permitted to protect property. But what if someone does not *use* deadly force but only *threatens* to use it? Suppose you find a trespasser encamped on your land. Ever mindful of the danger of adverse possession (property students remember!), you point a gun at the trespasser and tell him that, if he does not leave, you will kill him. You are charged with criminal assault. Do you have a defense of protection of property? Have you used "deadly force" in protection of property (no defense allowed) or only "non-deadly force" (defense allowed)?

Courts appear to be divided on this issue. Some take the view that as long as you do not shoot the gun, you have only used non-deadly force, and you may have a defense. Others worry that permitting such behavior encourages threats, which may escalate into violence, and thus do not allow such a defense.

What about after you have been dispossessed? The common law allows a person who has just been dispossessed of his property to follow the wrongful dispossessor in hot pursuit and use non-deadly force to get it back. But deadly force is not allowed. Does this mean that you cannot shoot to kill a mugger who flees after taking your wallet? Yes, although you could, presumably, shoot him in the leg to stop him from getting away with your wallet, and you could shoot to kill him if he posed a threat to your *life* as opposed to only a threat to your *property*.

What about defense of your home? The common law has

said, from time immemorial, that a "man's home is his castle."
As Sir Edward Coke put it in his *Institutes* of 1644, "where shall
a man be safe if not in his own home"?[6] Thus, when an intruder
enters your home, the common law says that more than your
property is at risk. The "castle" has been invaded; the "fortress"
has been breached.

Under the old common law rule, you were legally justified
in using *deadly* force to protect your home against any person
whom you reasonably believed was about to make an unlawful
entry into it, provided only that you reasonably believed such
force was necessary to prevent the unlawful intrusion. This rule
applied regardless of the fact that there was no threat to
property or to the lives of the inhabitants of the home. Thus,
under this rule, if you see an unarmed, drunken man wandering
into your house by mistake at night, you can shoot him dead,
even if you know he means no harm, as long as you reasonably
think killing him is the only way to prevent him from entering.
Not surprisingly, few courts today take this view.

Today, most courts take the view that you may use deadly
force to prevent an intrusion into your home only if you have
reason to believe that the intruder intends some kind of
felony — some courts require that it be a violent felony — in the
home. Thus, you would not be justified in shooting the unarmed
drunken man, but you would be justified in shooting a would-
be robber or kidnapper, especially if you had reason to believe
they were armed.

In real cases, the distinctions between defense of person,
defense of property, and defense of habitation often blur. For
example, suppose you wake up in the middle of the night to find
a masked man with a revolver in his hand removing the
television from your living room. If you shoot and kill him, the
court may say that your killing is justified because, even though
deadly force is never permitted to protect property (the television), it is permitted to protect your life (and the lives of your
family members) and to protect your home (especially from an
armed intruder).

4. Insanity.

a. Introduction.

Even if Winters did not have a valid claim of self-defense in the subway killing hypothetical, he may have a defense of insanity. In some respects, the defense of insanity is like self-defense. Ordinarily, it is an issue raised by the defense. The reason for the defense, as in self-defense, is that it is thought that the purposes of the criminal law would not be served by conviction of a person who acted when they were insane, any more than they would be served by conviction of one who acted in self-defense.

But there are important differences between the defense of insanity and the defense of self-defense. For one thing, insanity is, as we have seen, an *excuse* defense, while self-defense is *justification*. This means that, while for self-defense we are saying that the defendant's *act* is acceptable, for insanity we are saying that the act is reprehensible but the *actor* is not to blame.

Second, while insanity, like self-defense, is a "complete" defense, in the sense that, if you were insane at the time of the crime, you are not guilty of the crime at all, a finding of insanity, unlike self-defense, does not result in the defendant just "going home." Instead, commitment to a mental institution — often mandatory commitment — and possibly for a longer time than the defendant would have served in jail for the offense, is the usual result of a verdict of "not guilty by reason of insanity."

Third, while self-defense is usually only available in homicide prosecutions or prosecutions for assault and battery or attempted homicide, insanity can be a defense to any crime. In fact, recent studies show that 86% of insanity pleas are made in trials of non-violent offenses. Thus, one may have a defense of insanity if one is prosecuted for shoplifting or income tax evasion. Some courts will not allow such a defense for strict liability offenses like traffic violations, on the grounds that even lunatics who violate such laws should pay a criminal penalty.

Insanity is relevant in many areas of law outside criminal law. For instance, a person who is insane cannot make a valid will, or serve on a jury, or testify in court. The definition of insanity for each of these situations differs. What about in the criminal context?

There are at least three circumstances in which insanity can be an issue in criminal law:

1) A person cannot be tried if, because of insanity, he is not competent to stand trial. A person is not competent to stand trial if he cannot understand the nature of the case against him

or assist in his own defense. This does not mean that the defendant is pleading insanity to the criminal charge. It means only that he cannot be tried because he cannot discuss strategy with his counsel or confront his accusers or even testify on his own behalf. If the court finds that the defendant is not competent to stand trial, it will suspend the trial until he regains his competence. If this never happens, there will be no trial. The defendant will be committed to a mental institution, but only for so long as necessary to determine whether he could be made competent to stand trial. If it is determined that he cannot be, he must be released, or committed pursuant to *civil* commitment proceedings, whereby a person is generally only subject to commitment if he is dangerous to himself or to others.

2) Insanity can also be an issue because an insane person cannot be executed. This means that, even if you were sane at the time you committed the crime (so you do not have an insanity defense to the criminal charge) and you were sane at the time of trial (so you were competent to stand trial), you cannot be put to death if you *became insane* after trial. The Supreme Court has ruled that executing the insane is cruel and unusual punishment.[7]

3) Finally, insanity is also an issue in a criminal trial because a person cannot be convicted of a crime if he was insane when he committed it. This is the context in which we will consider insanity in this chapter: when is insanity a defense in a criminal trial?

b. **The Insanity Defense: History and Rationale**.

It has been said that "no feature of criminal law is more controversial than the defense of insanity."[8] Ever since the first insanity acquittal in Anglo-American history in England in 1505, courts have struggled with the definition of legal insanity, and commentators have debated the rationale of the defense and whether it should be abolished. In recent years, the controversy reached a new peak with the not guilty by reason of insanity verdict in the case of John Hinkley, the man charged with attempting to assassinate President Reagan in 1981.

Advocates of the insanity defense say that an insane person cannot be deterred from committing the crime, and that it is unfair and unjust to punish the insane. There is, they say, an important difference between mental illness and wickedness. A person who kills his mother in law because he thinks she is the

Ayatollah, for instance, should not be punished.

Opponents of the insanity defense say it is a "rich man's defense" because only very wealthy defendants can afford to pay the expert witnesses necessary to prove the claim. They also worry that juries have too hard a time understanding the vague terms in the definition of the defense, or distinguishing between persons who are to blame for their mental infirmity and those who are not.

Opponents also say the defense is often abused, by defendants who make fraudulent claims of insanity and then unjustly escape criminal punishment and go free. This criticism appears to have little empirical support, however. First, the insanity defense is rarely used. Second, it is rarely successful, especially with juries. In fact, juries tend to be so unsympathetic to the insanity defense, that defense lawyers often call it a "defense of last resort." Then too, while an insane person does escape criminal punishment, he can hardly be said to go free, since he may very well serve a longer term in the mental institution than he would ever have served in prison had he been convicted.

Another very important criticism of the insanity defense is based on the view that it requires the adoption of principles of psychiatry in law, and such principles are not in keeping with the legal way of understanding things. The lawyer, it is said, asks about justice. He assumes that man is morally responsible for his actions. The psychiatrist does not understand terms like justice or moral desert. He thinks in terms of disease and reactions to chemical imbalances in the body. For him, a "criminal" is a sick person; for the lawyer, he is accountable. Allowing the insanity defense, some critics argue, attempts a dangerous intermingling of these two perspectives. At best, they will not mix at all. At worst, the law will adopt the perspective of psychiatry and acquit people who willfully violated the law because of a theory that their conduct was determined by mental processes or illnesses beyond their control.

It is certainly true that, to a very large degree, criminal law is hostile to the deterministic philosophy of psychology or the other "helping professions" like sociology. After all, if a person can be put in prison for stealing a loaf of bread when starving or for committing larceny when he is the product of a broken home, then the law clearly does believe that free will is possible and that a person is not forced to do what he does by his socio-

economic circumstances. On the other hand, there does not seem to be anything wrong with saying that, although criminal law is based on the assumption that people are responsible for the consequences of the choices they make in life (and thus even a poor person who chooses to become a thief is morally responsible), still we should not punish someone who, through no fault of his own, is mentally infirm. Philosophers like Aristotle, who believed firmly in the possibility of free will, also insisted that a person who truly "cannot help" doing what he does, through no fault of his own, deserves pardon and pity rather than condemnation.

Some states *have* abolished the insanity defense. But they also provide by statute that evidence of insanity can be admitted to negate the mental state required for the crime. Thus, for example, if a man is accused of murdering his wife by strangulation, and the jury is satisfied that he did not know he was squeezing a human being's throat because he thought he was squeezing a lemon, the man will not be guilty, even in a state that has abolished the insanity defense, because his insanity will still show that he did not have the *mens rea* for the crime. It might well be unconstitutional for a state to say that evidence of insanity is not admissible for any purpose in a criminal trial, even to negate the existence of *mens rea*.

c. **Tests of Insanity**.

Over the years, the courts have formulated a number of different tests to determine whether a defendant was legally insane at the time he committed a crime. The tests are, in fact, quite different, although in practice, in many cases, the differences do not appear to affect the results.

1) **The M'Naghten Test**.

In 1843, in England, Daniel M'Naghten shot and killed the Secretary to the Prime Minister Sir Robert Peel.[9] M'Naghten mistakenly thought the Secretary was Peel, and also thought that Peel and the Tories were out to get him. At his trial, M'Naghten's lawyer pleaded insanity, and the jury found him not guilty by reason of insanity. The public outcry forced a debate in the House of Lords, which put five questions to the Justices of Queen's Bench. The answers to those questions were later appended to the report of the opinion in the case, and have since come to be treated as part of the opinion. From this

advisory opinion comes the famous M'Naghten test: a person is not guilty by reason of insanity if, at the time of the offense, he suffered from a *disease of the mind* which caused him not to know either the *nature and quality of his act* (what he was doing) or not to know that *what he was doing was wrong.*

Observe that this test has three parts. First, you must have a mental disease (or defect). Second, that mental disease must cause you to have a cognitive (knowledge) incapacity of one of two types. You are insane if the mental disease causes you not to know what you are doing — e.g., you are strangling your wife but you think you are squeezing a lemon. Or you can also be insane, even if you *do* know what you are doing, if you do not know that what you are doing is wrong.

A majority of states in the United States use the M'Naghten approach. Some supplement it, as we shall see, with the Irresistible Impulse Test. In the federal system, the McNaghten Rule was mandated by Congress in 1984, after the public outcry over the Hinkley verdict led to dissatisfaction with the model penal code approach.

Courts give very little guidance to juries on what the terms mean in this test. At least four terms in the test have given problems: "mental disease," "know," "nature and quality of the act," and, above all, "wrong." What does each of these terms mean?

There is no clear legal definition of mental disease, for M'Naghten or any of the other tests. And this may seem strange, since *all* tests of legal insanity require mental disease. No person can raise a defense of legal insanity in the United States unless, at the time of the offense, he suffered from a mental disease or defect.[10]

Some say the difficulty is that mental disease is not really a legal term at all; it is a psychiatrist's term. On the other hand, *insanity* is a *legal* term. That is why it is absolutely wrong to say that a person has a defense of mental disease in a criminal case. The defense is *insanity*, and the *law* defines insanity.

No person, as I have said, is insane unless he has a mental disease or defect. It is, however, possible for a person to have a mental disease and not be legally insane. If a person's mental disease does not interfere with his ability to know what he is doing or to know that what he is doing is wrong, he is not insane under M'Naghten. Still, what does "mental disease" mean?

Some courts and commentators take the view that only certain psychoses will qualify as mental diseases under M'Naghten. Certainly there is little doubt that a condition such as that of a psychopath is *not* a mental disease for these purposes. A person who merely performs repeated criminal or antisocial acts is not, thereby, suffering from a mental disease. But what about someone who is suffering from strange delusions?

It has been said that there "never has been a person who labors under partial delusion only and is not in other respects insane."[11] On the other hand, it seems possible to imagine a person who has delusions, but who seems perfectly capable, in other respects, of knowing what he is doing. Is such a person suffering from a mental disease? Is such a person insane?

The M'Naghten case itself involved such an individual, so the Justices had something to say about delusions in their answers to the House of Lords' questions. A delusional person, they noted,

> must be considered in the same situation as to responsibility as if the facts with respect to which the delusion exists were real. For example, if under the influence of his delusion he supposes another man to be in the act of attempting to take away his life, and he kills that man, as he supposes in self defense, he would be exempt from punishment. If his delusion was that the deceased had inflicted a serious injury on his character and fortune, and he killed him in revenge for such supposed injury, he would be liable to punishment.

This is a confusing passage. For one thing, it is arguable that it sets up a separate test for the insanity of delusional individuals. In other words, even if a delusional person knows what he is doing and knows that society regards it as wrong, he is not guilty if the facts which he imagined, if true, would make him not guilty of a crime. For another, it makes self-defense a subjective defense. As we saw in the previous chapter, most courts use an objective standard, requiring that the defendant's belief in the necessity to use deadly force be objectively reasonable.

Most courts and commentators examining the issue seem to conclude that there is no separate insanity test for delusional people under M'Naghten. There was no such test at the time of the M'Naghten case, and the Justices in their advisory opinion were really only trying to restate the law as it then existed. This means that a person is not insane, under M'Naghten, even if he suffers from a severe delusion, *unless* that delusion (which could, very well, be regarded as a mental disease) causes him not to know what he is doing or that what he is doing is wrong. On the other hand, he may be acquitted on grounds of insanity even if his delusion causes him to believe facts which, if true, would not be a defense. For instance, suppose that A has a delusion that B hates him. A poisons B and kills him. If A has a mental disease which causes him not to know that killing B is wrong, he will be acquitted on grounds of insanity even though the fact that he imagined, B's hating him, in no way excuses his behavior.

In short, with the exception of the psychopathic personality, practically any mental illness or defect, including delusions, can qualify as a "mental disease, but it will not make the person legally insane (and thus will not excuse his crime) unless it causes him not to know what he is doing or that what he is doing is wrong. But what does "know" mean?

Here, too, courts give juries practically no help. The problem is that, if the word only means "intellectual awareness," it seems unduly restrictive. Few mentally diseased people, it is said, are incapable of "knowing" what they are doing — in the sense that a child knows what he or she is doing. That is why, some say, the word "know" in this context requires a deeper meaning — an appreciation, an understanding. But the issue has not been resolved by the courts.

What does it mean to say that the defendant must have known "the nature and quality of his act" (or to have known "what he was doing")? Most courts seem to conclude that this means little more than knowledge of physical consequences. You are insane if you do not know that stabbing a person in the throat will likely cause them to die or that hitting a pane of glass hard with a hammer will likely cause it to break.

Someone who does not know what he is doing cannot, really, know it is wrong. If, for example, you do not know you are shooting a gun at someone, but think, instead, that the gun is a banana, you obviously cannot know that what you are doing is wrong. But, even if you *do* know what you are doing, you still may not know that what you are doing is "wrong." What does "wrong" mean in this context? This is the most difficult word in the M'Naghten test.

Suppose A kills B, knowing that killing is against the law, but also thinking that an angel of God came down to earth and commanded him to kill B. Does A "know" that killing B is "wrong"?

Suppose C kills D, knowing that killing is against the law, but also thinking that his religion commanded him to kill D. Does "know" mean "legal knowledge" or "moral knowledge"?

In England, "wrong" in the M'Naghten test is defined as *legal* wrong. A person is not insane, in other words, even if he has a mental disease, unless he does not know what he is doing or does not know his act is against the law. It does not matter if he thinks it is morally justifiable.

In America, courts are divided on the issue of moral versus legal wrong. But even courts requiring moral wrong tend to agree that it is *society's* definition of moral wrong that counts, not that of the individual. For instance, in the hypothetical above, A would not be insane even if he personally thought that it was right to kill B, as long as he knew that society generally regarded such an act as morally wrong. Since *society's* definition of *moral wrong* is, in many situations, likely to be the same as the definition of *legal* wrong, most American courts seem to treat "wrong" in the M'Naghten test as if it means "legal wrong."

2) The Irresistible Impulse Test.

One criticism often made of M'Naghten is that it is too focused on *cognitive* impairment — on the lack of the ability to *know* things. Mentally diseased people, it is said, frequently suffer from an impairment of *volitional* capacity: they know things, but cannot control themselves. Thus, a few states following the M'Naghten rule have *supplemented* it with what has, unfortunately, come to be called the "irresistible impulse test." In such states, a person is not guilty by reason of insanity, even if he does know what he is doing and does know it is wrong, if, because of mental disease, he was incapable of conforming to the law.

Like M'Naghten, this test is very old. It apparently originated, in Anglo-American legal history, in 1840 in a case in which a man called Oxford (no relation to the University) was accused of firing a pistol at Queen Victoria. The court said: "If some controlling disease was, in truth, the acting power within him which he could not resist, then he will not be responsible."[12]

I have said that the term "irresistible impulse" is unfortunate. This is because neither word is to be taken literally.

"Irresistible" does not mean *absolutely* irresistible. Although some courts, especially military courts, tend to follow the "policeman at the elbow" version of this test — you are insane if, because of mental disease, you would still have committed the crime even if a policeman were standing at your elbow — most courts seem to regard that approach as too extreme. Even people who would desist from acting if a policeman were at their elbow can have the sort of volitional incapacity needed to be acquitted under this test. Then too, *impulse* does not require a sudden act. A person may be acquitted of murder, under the irresistible impulse test, even if he planned the murder for weeks, as long as his mental disease forced him to take the action that he did and, essentially, robbed him of free will.

Critics of this test point out that it is dangerous to say a person is not guilty because he "could not help" doing what he did. Why, then, not acquit hungry people of stealing food, or unemployed people of robbing banks, or emotionally disturbed people of stabbing people with steak knives when they do not accept gifts of wine? We do not acquit such persons, it is said, because the law assumes that human beings can and should resist every unlawful impulse, however great.

3) **The Durham Test**.

Way back in 1871, New Hampshire became the first state to abolish the M'Naghten test. Influenced by the scholarly work of Dr. Isaac Ray, who believed that it is not possible to focus on only one part of an insane person's mind, such as his lack of cognitive or volitional ability, a New Hampshire court ruled that a person is not guilty by reason of insanity if "his crime was the offspring or product of mental disease."[13]

But this New Hampshire test proved an aberration. For over eighty years, no other state adopted it. Then in 1954, in the case of *Durham v. United States*, the United States Court of Appeals for the District of Columbia Circuit adopted it. Judge David Bazelon — who should be familiar to property students as one of the first judges to formulate the "implied warranty of habitability" rule in landlord-tenant law — wrote that "an accused is not criminally responsible if his unlawful act was the product of mental disease or defect."

The Durham test, as it has come to be called, is usually said to be the most favorable to the defense of all the insanity tests because it only requires proof of mental disease and a causative link between that mental disease and the act. It does not require that the defendant be unable to know anything, or unable to control his actions.

When the test was laid down in the *Durham* case, many praised it as expanding the area of inquiry beyond knowledge and volition. But many critics condemned it, saying it would make juries too dependent on psychiatrists and that if the causation required was to be "but for" causation, then a person would rarely be acquitted on grounds of insanity under this test, since it can rarely be said that a person would not have committed a particular act if he had not been suffering from a particular mental disease.

Critics also pointed out that it could acquit defendants unfairly. For instance, suppose A has a mental disease, which causes him to believe that his daughter hates him. He kills his daughter. Under the Durham test, he might be acquitted if a jury is satisfied that he has a mental disease, which caused his delusion and that he would not have killed his daughter if he did not have the disease or the delusion. But under the M'Naghten plus irresistible impulse test, he would not be acquitted unless he did not know that killing his daughter under these circumstances was wrong or unless he could not stop himself from doing so.

The DC Circuit decided over a hundred insanity cases in the ten years after *Durham*, trying to clarify the test. Problems emerged. In one case, a psychiatrist testified on a Friday that a particular mental condition was not a mental disease. Over the weekend, the psychiatrist's hospital made an administrative change in policy, which reclassified the condition as a mental disease.[14] In another case, a man was convicted of murder because the testifying psychiatrists said his condition was not a mental disease. A month later, the assistant superintendent at the hospital where these doctors practiced testified in a different case that he believed a condition like this is a mental disease. The defendant in the first case sought, and obtained, a retrial of his case.[15]

4) **The Model Penal Code Test**.

Under the Model Penal Code, a person is not guilty by reason of insanity if, as the result of mental disease or defect, he lacked substantial capacity *either*

(a.) to appreciate the criminality (wrongfulness) of his conduct

(b.) *or* to conform his conduct to the law

Notice that this test is like all the other tests in that it requires a mental disease or defect. Notice that it speaks of "substantial capacity." This is because the drafters specifically did not want to require a total lack of cognitive or volitional capacity, as the M'Naghten and irresistible impulse tests are *occasionally* said to require. Then too, the model penal code test uses the word appreciate instead of know, suggesting that appreciate means a deeper awareness than mere rote knowledge.

The most significant aspect of the Model Penal Code approach to insanity, however, is that it combines the M'Naghten and irresistible impulse tests without taking a position on the vexed question of whether "wrong" means moral wrong or legal wrong. That last issue is left to the states to work out for themselves. In a separate section, the Model Penal Code also expressly states that psychopathic (or repeated criminal) behavior is not mental disease.

Several states adopted the model penal code test. The federal courts did too, until Congress required them to go back to M'Naghten after the *Hinkley* verdict in 1984. Interestingly, the Congressional statute requires *severe* mental illness. But it does retain the Model Penal Code word "appreciate" instead of "know".

Today, a few states use the Model Penal Code approach, but more use M'Naghten, and the trend seems to be in favor of M'Naghten because it is believed to be harsher on criminals.

So much for defenses. Before concluding, we need to examine briefly another area of criminal law — crimes against property, which are generally subsumed under the broader heading of theft.

NOTES

1. Actually, self-defense is a specialized defense in that it usually can only be raised in prosecutions for criminal homicide or some level of criminal assault (or attempts at these crimes). Self-defense is never, of course, a defense to rape, and rarely if ever a defense to any form of theft, although necessity may be a defense to theft.

2. The Model Penal Code appears to reject the defense of inherently impossible attempts, although it recommends dismissal of the prosecution or a lower sentence if the facts show the defendant was not a public danger. For instance, a person who tries to kill another with a feather — assuming there is no insanity defense raised! — might be

convicted of and sentenced for attempted murder (provided he intended to kill and took a substantial step toward execution) because, if the facts had been as he believed them to be, he would have been able to kill his victim, and we cannot be sure that such a defendant will not, the next time, try using a gun or a knife instead of a feather. If there were evidence that he did not have such dangerous proclivities and would never try again with more serious means, the Model Code would recommend dismissal of the charge.

3. But Winters could still be guilty of a serious crime under the model penal code approach, as we will see shortly when we address the issue of "imperfect" self-defense.

4. *United States v. Peterson*, 483 F.2d at 1231.

5. Consider the implications of this last exception for battered wives who kill their husbands at home. The exception is based on the view that, when the attacker is also a rightful co-occupant of the home, the reason for not requiring retreat from the home — as in the situation where you are protecting the home from an intruder — is not present. But most courts take the view that the reason we do not require a person to retreat from his/her own home when attacked has nothing to do with the status of the assailant, but rather with the fact that there is no safer "castle" to retreat to. Thus, most courts applying the retreat rule do not require retreat from the home in any situation.

6. Coke, *Third Institute* 162 (1644), cited in Dressler, *Understanding Criminal Law*, p. 233.

7. Perhaps the most famous, or infamous, case of an insane person being executed is that of the assassin of President Garfield, who, apparently, went to the gallows in 1881 in a state of lunacy.

8. Dressler, *Understanding Criminal Law*, p. 289.

9. Consider this issue in light of the Aristotle discussion in my article on "Criminal Jurisprudence From Plato to Hegel," 39 *American Journal of Jurisprudence* 97-152 (1994).

10. Peel is also famous for originating the organized police force in Britain. Police officers in Britain are, to this day, called "bobbies" because of Robert Peel.

11. It is said that the difference between a mental disease and a mental defect is that a disease means a condition that can improve or get worse, while a defect refers to some permanent brain malfunction, like retardation. See Dressler, *Understanding Criminal Law*, p. 298.

12. See C. Merier, *Criminal Responsibility* (1928), cited in LaFave and

Scott, *Criminal Law*, p. 317.

13. *Regina v. Oxford*, 175 Eng. Rep. 941 (1840). But no mention was made of this doctrine in M'Naghten, and it was abolished in England as a "dangerous doctrine" in 1863.

14. *State v. Jones*, 50 NH 369 (1871).

15. See *In Re Rosenfield*, 157 F. Supp. 18, cited in Dressler, *Understanding Criminal Law*, p. 303.

16. See *Blocker v. United States*, 288 F2d 853 (DC Cir., 1961), cited in LaFave and Scott, p. 328.

CHAPTER THIRTEEN

Crimes Against Property

The Seventh Commandment states, "Thou shalt not steal." From time immemorial, men have, by an almost infinite variety of ways, sought to acquire the property of others. When are such actions criminal?

In ancient times, most infringements on the property of others were dealt with under the law of torts, not under criminal law, so that only damages was the remedy.[1] Under the early English common law, by contrast, theft was a felony, and punishable by death. This continued to be true of the law of England until the early 1800s. Partly because of the harshness of this sentence, English judges construed the elements of theft offenses very narrowly, so as to avoid imposing the death penalty too often. A good many of the fine distinctions still characteristic of the law of theft stem from this historical fact.

Three major theft offenses emerged from English law over the years. The first, larceny, is a felony created by the common law. The other two, embezzlement and false pretenses, were misdemeanors created by Parliament to remedy perceived inadequacies in the way larceny was restrictively interpreted by the courts. Rules of pleading were very strict; courts required that the state indict for one crime only, and prove that offense exactly or lose the case.[2]

Today, under the Model Penal Code as well as the statutory law of most states, all three of these theft offenses have been consolidated into one single crime, theft, which can be committed in a variety of ways and which can be either a felony or a misdemeanor, usually depending on the value of the property taken. In this chapter, I will concentrate on the common law elements of the theft offenses because those elements are frequently tested on the bar exam, and because even today important remnants of this common law system remain in virtually all states.

1. Larceny.

Larceny requires several elements. There must be: (a) a **trespassory** (b) **taking and *carrying away* (*asportation*)** (c) of the ***personal property*** (d) of ***another*** (e) with ***intent*** to ***deprive him of it permanently*** (or for a long period of time).

a. trespassory

Trespassory means that the defendant must *not* have already obtained lawful possession of the item. For instance, suppose Max loans Fred his Mercedes for the day. After driving it around the block a few times, Fred decides to keep it and he never returns it to Max. Is Fred guilty of common law larceny? No, because he had rightful possession of the car initially. His initial taking of it was not a trespass.

Larceny is always a taking from one in *possession*. What does possession mean? Here a little knowledge of property law is helpful. Possession is not the same as *title*. A person who has title to a house or car does not have possession if he has leased it to someone else. Possession is also not the same thing as *custody*, which means a momentary physical control of an item, subject to the right of the owner to regain it at any time. As used in criminal law, possession usually means the legal right to control an object physically for a reasonably long time.

Consider the following examples:

1) Friedrick takes his car to the repair shop. The shop fixes the car, but Friedrick refuses to pay the bill. Instead, Friedrick just takes the car home without the shop owner's permission. Friedrick may be guilty of common law larceny, because the court may say

that the shop had a *possessory* lien on the car. Friedrick was trespassing on their possessory rights.

2) Professor Pauley hands his wallet to one of his students to hold for a minute while he carries a huge pile of Xeroxed copies into his criminal law class. The student absconds with the wallet. The student is probably guilty of common law larceny, because Pauley never surrendered possession of the wallet, only custody to him.

3) Professor Pauley gives his student his wallet to hold for a week while he is vacationing in Afghanistan. The student keeps the wallet and does not return it. The student is probably not guilty of common law larceny (he is, of course, guilty of some other crime, see below), because he had lawful possession of the wallet when he decided to keep it permanently.

4) A thief steals Mabel Gloag's diamond ring and gets on the London Tube with it. Professor Pauley takes the ring from the thief's pocket and keeps it. Pauley is probably guilty of common law larceny, even though he stole from a thief, because a thief has superior *possessory* rights to the property over every person in the entire world *except* the true owner (Mabel).

These rules may have suited a time when property transactions were face to face. By the fifteenth and sixteenth centuries, however, English merchant adventurers were trading around the globe, and new problems of theft emerged.

In *The Carrier's Case* in 1473, a London dealer hired the defendant to carry some packages for him to the port of Southampton. The defendant got about half-way on his journey, and then broke open the packages and hid the contents, keeping them for himself. When caught and prosecuted, he claimed it was not larceny because he already had possession of the packages. The court agreed, but it held him guilty of larceny anyway. The defendant had possession of the packages, but only of the packages, not of the goods inside. When he "broke bulk" and took the *contents* of the packages, he trespassed on the possessory rights of the dealer, and thus was guilty of larceny.

This was only the first of many fictions that gradually helped modify some of the harshness of the common law crime of larceny. Routine employees are not said to have possession of their employer's goods when they are in the employer's building or when they are given physical control of the items by the employer. Instead, they have *custody*, and the employer retains *constructive* possession. For instance, suppose a janitor takes home the mop he uses to clean the floor, or suppose a bank teller takes money from a customer, puts it in the bank cash drawer, and then later removes it and takes it home. The janitor and the teller would both be guilty of common law larceny, because they trespassed on their employer's constructive possession of the items.

On the other hand, suppose it is a high level employee who takes something — for instance, a senior vice president takes the telephone in his office. Or suppose the bank teller does not put the money in the cash drawer; instead, he takes it from the customer and puts it in his pocket. Then, courts will say this is *not* larceny, because the employer never had possession of the item. The senior vice president had possession of the telephone. The bank teller acquired possession of the money from the client.

Suppose you *find* property and keep it without trying to contact the true owner. Is that larceny? Does the finder have possession? Here too, the courts developed a legal fiction. If the owner has *mislaid* the property (intentionally put it down somewhere and forgotten about it) <u>or</u> if the owner has *lost* the property (unintentionally lost possession of it) but there is a clue to its ownership, the owner is said to retain constructive possession of the item. Thus, if the finder just keeps it and makes no effort to locate the owner, he may well be guilty of larceny. On the other hand, if the property is *abandoned*, or if there is no clue as to its ownership, a person who finds it is not guilty of larceny, even if he decides, then and there, to keep it.

b. **taking and carrying away (asportation)**

Asportation just means that, to be guilty of larceny, the defendant must have physically moved the item. Even a change of position of a few inches is sufficient. For instance, a shoplifter who throws an item of personal property into his bag in a store has taken and carried away the item.

c. **of the *personal* property**

Only personal property may be the subject of common law larceny. In fact, common law courts held that larceny only applies to *tangible* personal property of value. For instance, checks, bonds, and services of various kinds are not subject to common law larceny. Under old English law, domestic pets like cats and dogs could not be the subject of common law larceny because they were of no significant value. On the other hand, cows, horses, and pigs could be, because they were valuable.

What about real property? Land and houses could not be the subject of common law larceny because they could not be "carried away." What of fixtures on the land? Here, the law introduced a paradox. Suppose Sam cuts down five cedar trees on Tim's land and takes them home. Has Sam committed larceny? If he takes the trees as soon as he cuts them down, the common law says there is no larceny, because the trees are still part of the real property. But if Sam cuts them down, and then goes home to rest for a while and comes back and takes the trees, that is larceny because the trees became personal property in the interim.

d. of another

Suppose Simon Spaulding wrongly believes that Felix Cameron's Mercedes belongs to him, so he takes it. Simon is *not* guilty of larceny, even if his belief is not reasonable, because he does not "know" that the Mercedes belongs to another. He has a defense of mistake of fact, or a "claim of right."

e. with intent to deprive them of it permanently

Larceny requires an intent to steal. An intent to deprive a person of his property for an unreasonable period of time is equivalent to an intent to steal. What is an unreasonable period of time? It depends on the nature of the property, and it may also depend on what I know about what you are planning to do with it. If I take your car without your permission with intent to return it in an hour, that is probably not an intent to steal. But if I know you will need the car during that hour to get to an important meeting, it might be an intent to steal, because I am intending to deprive you of a significant possessory right, the right to use the car during that hour.

Suppose I take your car with intent to abandon it somewhere where you will never find it, or to destroy it. Do I have an intent to steal? Under the common law, yes. The focus, in other words, is on the loss to the possessor, not the gain to the taker. The taker has an intent to steal even if he has no intention of keeping or using the item he takes.

What if I take your car with intent to use it in a demolition-derby, and then return it to you after that? Is that an intent to steal? The courts say that if my belief that I could return the item to you in its original form was unreasonable, there was an intent to steal.

Even though my subjective intent was not to deprive you of the car permanently, I should have known (negligence) that I probably would not be able to do so, given what I intended to do with it.

Suppose that when I take your car without your permission, I intend only to borrow it from you for an hour, during which time I believe you do not need it. *After* borrowing it, I decide to keep it permanently. Am I guilty of larceny?

The old common law courts said no. They imposed a requirement: the taking and the intent to deprive permanently had to be *contemporaneous* (at the same time) or there was no larceny. But gradually the courts thought this was unfair, so they developed the doctrine of continuing trespass. Since my original taking of the car was trespassory (I borrowed it without your permission), that trespass continues as long as I keep the borrowed car. If I then form the intent to *keep* the borrowed car, the intent to deprive permanently and the trespass *are* simultaneous, and thus I am guilty of larceny.

But suppose I *did* have your permission to borrow the car initially, and later I formed the intent to keep it? That is *not* larceny because my original taking was not trespassory. Suppose a bank teller accepts money from a customer at the bank, and puts it in his pocket instead of in the bank's cash drawer, intending to use it to fly away to Mexico and live in luxury. That is *not* larceny because there is no trespass on the possessory right of another. He does not wrongfully take it from the possession of the customer because the customer *gives* him the money. He does not wrongfully take it from the possession of the bank because the bank never had possession. What crime is the bank teller guilty of?

2. Embezzlement

Embezzlement is the fraudulent *conversion* of the personal property of another by one who is *already in lawful possession* (not just custody) of it. The difference between larceny and embezzlement is that larceny requires taking *from* someone who has a superior possessory interest, whereas embezzlement is committed *by* someone who already has a right to possession.

Fraudulent means the defendant must intend to convert the property of another. As with larceny, it is a defense if the defendant, however unreasonably, truly believes that the property is his own.

Conversion means seriously interfering with the owner's rights to the property. It can involve using it for an unreasonably long period of time, damaging it, or withholding possession.

How do we know whether the defendant was already in lawful possession of the item? If the defendant originally took the item without the permission of the owner or possessor, he is not in lawful possession and the crime must be larceny, not embezzlement.

But suppose the defendant already has some rightful control of the item when he converts it to his own use. Here it depends on whether the control was possession or merely custody. If it is possession, the crime is embezzlement; if custody, it is larceny.

Consider the following examples:

a. A janitor takes the broom he uses at work to clean the floor. The janitor, "low level" employee, only had *custody*, not possession, of the broom. Therefore, the employer had possession. Therefore, there was a trespass on the *possessory* rights of another. Therefore, the janitor is guilty of larceny.

b. A senior vice president at the investment firm of Merrill, Lynch, Pierce, Fenner, and Ziggypuss, takes the clock off his office wall and brings it home, keeping it. The vice president, a "high level employee," probably had *possession* (not just custody) of the clock, so there was *no* trespass on the possessory rights of another. But he did *convert* the property to his own use. He is guilty of embezzlement.

c. A bank teller takes money from a customer and puts it in the cash drawer. A few hours later, he removes it and takes it home. The crime is larceny because the bank had possession of the money when it was in the drawer, and he wrongfully took it from the bank's possession.

d. Same facts as above, except that the teller does *not* put it in the drawer. He accepts it from the customer and immediately puts it in his pocket. The crime is embezzlement because he initially had lawful possession of the item, and he then converted that possession, wrongfully, into permanent use.

e. Sam borrows Jack's Jaguar *without* Jack's permission, intending to return it in an hour. During the hour, Sam decides to keep the car. This is larceny under the doctrine of continuing trespass. The initial borrowing was trespassory.

f. Same facts as above, except that Sam borrows the car *with* Jack's permission, intending to return it, as agreed, in an hour. Sam then decides to keep the car. This is embezzlement, because Sam had lawful possession of the car, and then converted it to his own permanent use.

3. *Larceny by Trick and Taking By False Pretenses*

Suppose I ask you if I can borrow your car for an hour. In fact, my intent at the time I ask you is to sell the car and never return it to you. Is this larceny or embezzlement? One is tempted to say that it is not larceny, because I obtained lawful possession of the car (you gave it to me) before I converted it (sold it). But you did not give it to me *voluntarily*. I tricked you into it by lying to you that I was going to return it in an hour. This is larceny by trick. The possessor has given possession of the item to the defendant, but he has done so only because of a defendant's trick. The trick vitiates the consent. There was an unlawful trespass on the possessory rights of another.

Suppose instead that I ask you to *give* or *sell* me your car, by lying to you that I need it to take my ailing aunt to the hospital. If you *do* give or sell me the car because of my lie, the courts treat this as a different crime on my part: obtaining property under false pretenses. This crime requires a *representation* of a false present or past *fact*, which the defendant *knows* to be false, and which he *intends* will and *does* cause the victim to transfer *title* to the property to the defendant.

The defendant must *know* that the representation is false. And the representation must, in fact, be false. Even if the defendant believes it is false, there is no false pretenses crime unless the representation is in fact false. Any words or conduct can constitute the representation, but silence is not enough unless the seller has some special fiduciary duty to the buyer.

The representation must be of a past or present fact. A *promise* is not a representation, even if I never intend to keep it. A *prediction* of a future event ("this car will last for at least 10 years") is not a representation, even if I know it will not happen.

An expression of opinion ("puffing": "this is the best car money can buy") is not a representation, even if I know it is false.

The representation must *cause* the victim to rely on it and to pass *title* to the defendant. If the victim knows the representation is false but passes title anyway, there is no false pretenses crime. If the victim only gives the defendant *possession* and not *title*, the crime is larceny by trick, not false pretenses. And the defendant must *intend to defraud* the victim. As with larceny, if the defendant believes, however unreasonably, that he in fact owns the property or has a legal right to it, there is no crime of false pretenses.

Suppose I intentionally give you a bad check. Most courts hold that when you give someone a check, that is an implied representation that you have sufficient funds in the bank to meet the amount of the check. If there are not sufficient funds and you know this, and the victim, relying on your check, gives you title to the property, you are guilty of false pretenses. If the victim only gives you possession (loans you the property), the crime is larceny by trick. If the check is postdated, there is no false pretenses because there is no false representation of a past or present fact: in effect, you are *predicting* that you will have sufficient funds in the bank on the date of the check, and that is not false pretenses even if you know it cannot possibly happen.

4. The Model Penal Code and Other Crimes Against Property

The Model Penal Code provides for one crime of "theft," which can be committed in various ways — including larceny or embezzlement or false pretenses. Theft, under the Code, may also be accomplished by extortion. Under the common law, extortion meant that a public official corruptly received a fee for services which should have been rendered gratuitously. Under modern statutory law, however, extortion usually means the use of threat of future injury to obtain the property of another. Under the Model Penal Code, a person is guilty of theft by extortion if he purposely obtains property of another by threatening to inflict bodily injury on anyone, or commit any other criminal offense, or expose any secret tending to subject someone to hatred or ridicule, or otherwise to inflict any other kind of serious harm.

If the threat is not of *future* injury but of *present* injury, the law calls the crime robbery. Robbery, under the common law, is larceny from the person of another by force or threat of force. All the elements of larceny must be present. Larceny is also a lesser included offense of robbery, so a person cannot be convicted of *both* larceny and robbery for the same taking of property. To say that the larceny must be "from the person of another" does not mean the victim must be actually holding the property at the time it is taken. It is enough that the victim is or should be able to reach or control it. If a thief enters a house and locks the owner in the closet while he steals the television set, the taking is said to be "from the person" of the owner, and thus there is robbery. If a store-owner is held at gun-point while the thief opens the cash drawer and removes the money, the taking is "from the person" and thus there is robbery.

Robbery requires force or threat of immediate force. If a mugger snatches a woman's handbag by surprise and without a struggle, there is no robbery, only larceny, even if the mugger later uses force to prevent the owner from getting it back. If there is a fight for it, there is robbery. What counts is the victim's *fear*. Even if the gun the thief points is not loaded and the thief knows it, there is robbery if the victim believes it is loaded.

In addition to robbery and extortion and the other common law forms of theft, the Model Penal Code includes the offense of receiving stolen goods (which generally requires that the goods in fact be stolen *and* that the defendant knows they are stolen) under the rubric of theft offenses. Most important, the Code, and most states today, allow flexible pleading in theft cases: if the state indicts for theft by larceny, and the facts at trial prove theft by embezzlement or by false pretenses or robbery or extortion, the case will be tried under those facts and the defendant may be convicted of that crime.

There are some other important differences in the Code. The Code does not require "asportation" or moving of the property for any form of theft. All property, including real estate, can be the subject of theft under the Code. The focus, in the Code, is on the gain to the taker, not the harm to the possessor: if the taker intends to and does only destroy the property, not keep or sell it, the crime is not theft, under the Code, but "criminal mischief."

The Code also includes all promises about future action as representations for the purpose of the crime of theft by false pretenses. And the code rejects the common law rule that one cannot steal from one's spouse.

NOTES

1. There were some exceptions. Theft of a bather's clothes and theft of

livestock, for example, were punished as crimes in ancient Rome.

2. See *Criminal Law* by Richard Singer and John La Fond (Aspen Law and Business, 1997), p. 207.

CHAPTER FOURTEEN

Conclusions

We have now considered the fundamentals of all crimes — *actus reus* and *mens rea*. We have examined in detail a wide range of offenses, from all degrees of criminal homicide to group crimes like conspiracy and aiding and abetting and various types of theft. We have also explored a number of defenses, including insanity, self-defense, defense of property and habitation, and both mistake of fact and mistake of law.

Certainly this overview does not exhaust the scope of criminal law. For instance, although we touched on *causation* when considering felony murder, there is a great deal more that could be said on both but-for and proximate causation. There are also *other crimes* of great importance, including rape, which the United States Supreme Court has called the "ultimate violation of self," short of homicide. Finally, there is the whole topic of sentencing and punishment. Why do we punish criminals, is it for deterrence, retribution, rehabilitation, or some other reason? Is capital punishment a fit penalty for a brutal serial killer or a mass murderer like Timothy McVeigh? Or is the death penalty a barbarous anachronism in a twentieth-century society?

There are, of course, many very good books on punishment. For an introductory overview, my article on "Criminal Jurisprudence From Plato to Hegel" (39 *American Journal of Jurisprudence*, 1994) surveys some of the leading approaches and examines their roots in classical and early modern philosophy. And there are many other more comprehensive books on criminal law, a number of which are recommended in the selected bibliography at the back of this book.

For any topics not covered here, however, the analysis I have been stressing is largely the same. For nearly all crimes, there will be an *actus reus* and a *mens rea*. The same issues of intent, duty, defenses, and mistake recur in all areas of criminal law. This book thus provides the necessary foundation for all future study of the subject, whether in school or in the office of a judge, prosecutor, or defense counselor.

But does the book do more than this? Can we draw any conclusions about criminal law in contemporary America? Certainly we face a criminal justice crisis in our country. Indeed, as the twenty-first century approaches, more and more Americans see crime as a "clear and present danger" to the safety of our people and our whole way of life. Our city streets are not safe from murderers and violent gangs; drug related crimes are rampant; there are now threats of terrorism on our shores. What should America as a sovereign nation do about these problems? Should we change our legal definitions of crimes like murder, manslaughter, and assault? Should we continue to treat certain conditions, like insanity, as complete defenses, while regarding others, like poverty, as no defense at all?

This book can help start us thinking about questions like these. In the last analysis, however, we need to recognize that criminal law cannot do the whole job of social control. As Roscoe Pound taught many years ago in *Criminal Justice in America*, criminal law is only part of the answer. Religion, education, social mores — a wide variety of things are needed to restrain man's tendency to fall into the habit of vice.

Does this mean that if we improved these other social aids, criminal law and punishment might some day no longer be needed? Some contemporary commentators seem to think so. Like Marx, they look forward to the day when, with the end of capitalism, the alienation of man in society will also end, and crime itself and the need to punish will vanish. But the ancient philosophers taught us long ago that this will never be possible. In *The Laws*, Plato suggests that crimes will always be with us because of "our universal human frailty." After all, the Athenian asks Clinias in Book IX of that dialogue, why do we need criminal law if we have so ordered the educational and social system so that men will "enjoy all the right conditions for the practice of virtue"? But the Athenian answers his own question: "we are but men," and criminal punishment is a necessary remedy for the "slips of humanity." Aristotle agrees, saying in his *Politics* that just punishments "are good only because we cannot do without them [and] it would be better that neither individuals nor states should need anything of the sort."

For Plato and Aristotle, then, as indeed for twentieth-century America, criminal law is a necessary evil. It is only a *part* of law, but it is a part without which all human law is not possible and cannot be understood.

Selected Bibliography

Dressler, Joshua. *Cases and Materials on Criminal Law.* St. Paul: West Publishing Co., 1994.

Dressler, Joshua. *Understanding Criminal Law.* New York: Matthew Bender, 1987/1995.

Kadish, Sanford and Schulhofer, Stephen. *Criminal Law and Its Processes.* Sixth Edition. Boston: Little Brown/Aspen, 1995.

LaFave, Wayne and Scott, Austin W., Jr. *Criminal Law.* Second Edition. St. Paul: West Publishing Co., 1986.

Loewy, Arnold H. *Criminal Law in a Nutshell.* St. Paul: Nutshell Series of West Publishing Company, 1987.

Robinson, Paul H. *Criminal Law.* New York: Aspen Law and Business, 1977.

Singer, Richard G. and LaFond, John Q. *Criminal Law: Examples and Explanations.* New York: Aspen Law and Business, 1997.